Use of Government Publications by Social Scientists

This book is the first in the series
LIBRARIES AND LIBRARIANSHIP
An International Series
edited by
Melvin J. Voigt
University of California, San Diego
Evelyn H. Daniel
Syracuse University
Eldred Smith
University of Minnesota

Use of Government Publications by Social Scientists

Peter Hernon
Simmons College

Ablex Publishing Corporation
Norwood, New Jersey 07648

Printed in the United States of America.

Library of Congress Cataloging in Publication Data

Hernon, Peter.
    Use of government publications by social
scientists.

    (Libraries and librarianship)
    Based on author's thesis, Indiana University,
1978.
    Bibliography: p.
    Includes index.
    1. Government publications—Use studies.
2. Libraries—Special collections—Government
publications.   3. Libraries, University and college
—Use studies.   I. Title.   II. Series.
Z688.G6H47   025.17'3   79-16144
ISBN   0-89391-024-4

ABLEX Publishing Corporation
355 Chestunut Street
Norwood, New Jersey 07648

Contents

Appendices

Tables

Preface

Many of the depository libraries that receive official publications of the United States Government distributed through the Office of the Superintendent of Documents are the libraries of academic institutions. Although the items are normally received gratis, they cost the recipient libraries in terms of processing, storing, and handling of indexing-abstracting and loose-leaf services. Concerned about costs, many librarians believe that their collections of government publications are not utilized to their potential. To support this belief, they rely on circulation statistics, surveys, and, most often, personal opinion. There are many possible reasons for underutilization. Government publications are not under good bibliographic control. Researchers, students, and faculty may experience difficulty in becoming aware of, and gaining access to, needed government publications, even those held by the library. But these and other factors have had little systematic research.

All phases of government publications, from their production and distribution to their servicing and use in libraries, present major problems and issues amenable to research and investigation. However, many of the operating principles and conventions commonly accepted by documents librarians and educators are based on opinions and assumptions rather than on scientific investigation.

Many of the presently debated issues, such as those relating to depository systems and access to government information, have been discussed for decades and are apparently no closer to resolution than they were when they first arose. An examination of the literature shows that some aspects of library development, activities, and concerns have made little progress; for example, the arguments assessing the value of *separate* document collections versus *integrated* collections were formulated and solidified by the decade of the 1940s. Since then, "little has been done to transform the debate from an argument over conflicting opinions and assumptions to a disagreement over the interpretation of scientific data" (Waldo, 1977, 328).

"The purpose of research is to discover answers to questions through the application of scientific procedures" (Selltiz, Jahoda, Deutsch, & Cook, 1959, p. 2). In the process, opinions and assumptions may be found untenable, and more satisfactory approaches, in terms of costs, tieme, and results, derived. Research on questions relating to government documents may not necessarily result in problem solving or abate disagreement; but, as in other areas, it does add to knowledge, clarifies issues, and creates an awareness of unforeseen areas which merit further investigation.

The literature of librarianship contains an extensive body of writing about the publications of Federal, state, and municipal government. Yet, many of these are provincial and redundant, fulfilling a service function or conveying a particular viewpoint. The writings on municipal government publications, for example, suggest that the major concerns in the field have been related to bibliographic control, acquisition, distribution, depository systems and legislation, union lists of holdings, exchange programs, reference use, the value of these publications, the identification of bibliographic aids, bibliographies listing municipal publications, and classification and cataloging. Yet this literature is rarely based on research findings and usually does not analyze the informational needs of actual or potential users.

Except for literature describing reference sources or the value of documents in reference work, documents reference service in academic libraries is among the many topics that have received little scholarly attention. Even the "Guidelines for the Depository Library System" do not reflect a major concern for reference service. Depository libraries are encouraged to promote the use of the documents collection and to have "recognized focal points for inquiries about government publications," at which it should be possible to receive: "answers to reference questions or a referral to a source or place where answers can be found," and "guidance on the use of the collection" (U.S. Government Printing Office, 1977, pp. 5-7). Coverage of reference work, however, lacks the detail found in other sections of the guidelines.

There is a need for studies which compare the effectiveness of separate collections with that of integrated collections, analyze student utilization patterns, and investigate the reference interview and the referral process between general reference and documents departments. Answers to fundamental questions relating to public service should have an effect on the outcome of the reference interview and on encouraging patron willingness to request assistance. What are the implications for libraries of having separate collections or of organizing the material so that users must rely on assistance from library staff to find desired materials? Where public card catalogs indicate that particular publications are located in special document collections, can it be assumed that users are able to interpret the location symbols used and find the desired sources? Studies are also needed which focus on perceptual questions, such as any patrons' hesitancy in requesting assistance.

Thus, research topics abound in the field of documents reference service, many of which overlap and interact. An understanding of the reasons for faculty use and non-use of government publications can serve as a basis upon which many such topics can be studied. A cross-institutional analysis of faculty use and non-use provides the foundation for a comparative study of student utilization. In addition, studies of use and non-use are necessary because many academic libraries are finding that they can no longer accommodate rapidly expanding collections of government publications and must establish clear rationales for selecting those materials specifically needed by their clientele.

The cross-institutional study of faculty use and non-use of government publications, which forms the basis for this book, documents the importance that social scientists place upon government publications for teaching and research. The study provides data which should be of value in assisting the Government Printing Office in keeping its publication program and depository system attuned to the needs of an important segment of its user community. Also, the results should enable academic libraries to better structure their documents organization and service programs in the best interests of their patrons. Comparative data among institutions also provide insights into the functioning of the depository system in institutions that have various types of degree programs.

Acknowledgments

Since the study of documents use and non-use on which much of this book is based was investigated to fulfill the requirements for the Doctor of Philosophy degree, I would like to thank Dean Bernard M. Fry, Chairman of my dissertation committee, for his patient and valuable counsel. His influence on me extends far beyond completion of the dissertation. Appreciation is also due other members of the dissertation committee (Dr. David Clark, Dr. David Kaser, Professor Clayton Shepherd, and Dr. George Whitbeck) for their helpfulness, understanding, and friendship. The cooperation of those faculty members and librarians who participated in this study is greatly appreciated.

I am grateful to Elinor, Alison, and Linsay Hernon for their patience and understanding. They were very supportive while the dissertation and the subsequent book were being prepared. And, last, my parents, Robert and Ethel, who encouraged my pursuit of education.

Use of Government Publications
by Social Scientists

1. Use and Non-Use of Government Documents

THE PROBLEM OF DOCUMENT USE

Until relatively recent times, very little of the information produced by and related to governments has been made available, other than in centrally located archives. Today, with the greater complexity of modern society and the role government plays in most areas of human activity, wide dissemination of large blocks of such information has become essential. Governments acquire and disseminate information in practically every field of endeavor, and providing for many of the informational needs of citizens has become one of the expected services of government. Most of the information is in printed form, can be found in a wide variety of formats, and varies in quality; regardless, it has become essential for a variety of needs in education, the professions, business, recreation, research, and every-day living. Many of the publications issued by governments are distributed directly to those requiring or requesting them, but for the bulk of the material, and for retrospective study of government and its activities, users are dependent on document collections in libraries.

The acquisition and servicing of government information require extensive commitments on the part of libraries. It is imperative, therefore, that the reasons for use and non-use of government publications[1] be investigated. Many libraries purchase expensive indexing-abstracting services, bibliographies, and sets and compilations to ease access to diverse government publishing. It is important, especially in view of present budgetary restrictions, that librarians be able to

---

[1] *Government publications* refers to informational matter which is published as an individual document at government expense or as required by law (44 *U.S.C.* 1901).

1

justify the expenses involved in providing these services. How much are government documents used in teaching and research in colleges and universities, and how can such use be expanded and improved?

This book is based on a study designed to discover the reasons for the use and non-use of Federal, state, and municipal government publications by social scientists in college and university departments of economics, history, political science, and sociology. Scholars contacted were associated with selected academic institutions having degree programs ranging from the baccaluareate to the doctorate, having libraries holding Federal depository status, and situated within the states of Illinois, Indiana, Michigan, and Ohio.

Documents use is an area in which little research has been reported. It is true that "the number of use studies being conducted in libraries throughout the world has continued to increase over the years. From 1960 to 1973, a total of 477 articles were indexed in *Library Literature* under the heading of 'Use Studies'." However, an analysis of the 145 studies dealing with academic libraries reveals that important areas of library usage, such as the use of government publications, have received little attention. (Tobin, 1974, 101-113). As one library educator noted

> Studies are needed which consider the use of all types of government publications, not just federal publications. The little research in this area that has been done suggests some variation in use between state and federal documents, but more study of the differences in use patterns is needed. (Weech, 1978, 183)

Perhaps the most significant research finding to date suggests that although faculty members, to some extent, do use documents, most of their use is infrequent. It appears from existing evidence that documents use among faculty is not keeping pace with the increasing emphasis given them by governments, librarians, and commercial publishers.

The study on which this book is based investigated the reasons for academic use and non-use of Federal, state, and municipal government publications by full-time social science faculty members in selected colleges and universities. The study did not include the use of publications of foreign governments and international organizations, nor the use made of documents by undergraduate and graduate students, topics which may merit similar analysis. Emphasis was on faculty members, not only because of their own use or non-use of documents, but also because they heavily influence student utilization of library resources. Social scientists were selected for study because governments produce a vast amount of material relevant to their professional needs and because the social sciences, according to past surveys (discussed in Chapter 2), comprise the major user group for government publications.

Conclusions drawn from this study on document utilization should assist librarians in decision making related to the organization and servicing of government publications. An important determination is the degree of importance that social science faculty members place upon government publications as a resource for teaching and research. At the same time, patterns of non-use, faculty opinions about the quality of the information contained in documents, the extent of user satisfaction with the documents collection, and possible misconceptions about the relevance of documents for particular needs are also important. Librarians can analyze the accumulated data and determine whether to implement programs designed to correct any misconceptions, seek out and orient faculty members who would benefit from increased use of documents, and publicize the collection more effectively. Promoting greater library user awareness of the government documents collection should be a priority goal of depository libraries. One documents librarian feels that

> . . . Whether or not government documents are fully cataloged, with or without subject analytics, and distributed throughout the library or maintained as a separate collection, it is important that every means possible be directed to publicizing the information riches contained in public documents. (Reynolds, 1975, 288)

Suggestions for increasing the utilization of documents are included in the final chapter of this book.

The analysis of document utilization by social science faculty members in this study was confined to a subset of those academic libraries which have Federal depository status. Once designated, depository libraries are eligible to receive publications deemed by the Superintendent of Documents to be of sufficient public interest to warrant such distribution. The purpose of the depository system is to make government publications widely available. In fiscal year 1973, 12,490,228 copies of Federal government documents were distributed to depository libraries. By 1977 the number distributed had increased to 27,500,000.

Over the years the number of depository libraries has increased. For example, there were 1,054 depositories in fiscal year 1971, 1,084 in 1972, and 1,121 in 1973 (Annual Report of the Public Printer. Fiscal Year 1973. P. 28). By October 1975 the number had expanded to 1,186 and by mid-1978 had reached 1,217. Of these, approximately two-thirds are academic libraries, ranging from universities to small liberal arts colleges and community colleges; they include private as well as public institutions.

With these facts in mind, the objectives of the study were:

1. To depict the patterns of use by faculty of general library use as compared to their specific use of the government documents collection.
2. To depict the reasons for faculty use of government publications.
3. To depict the reasons for faculty non-use of government publications.
4. To relate the distribution of faculty on the descriptive characteristics to the federal depository library variables (see Fig. 1-1).

The study was carried out through questionnaires and interviews involving social science faculty members in colleges and universities and through question-

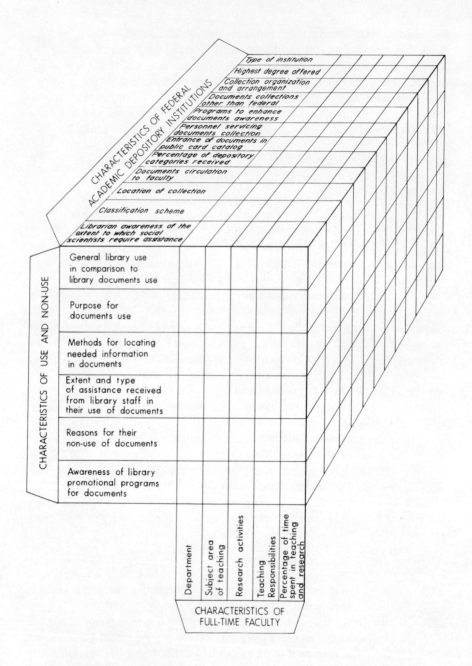

Figure 1-1   Characteristics of Use and Non-Use, Federal Academic
Depository Institutions, and Full-Time Faculty

naires to the libraries involved. The findings are summarized below and reported in more detail in Chapters 4 and 5.

A number of hypotheses have been formulated and tested relating both to the faculty and their use of documents and to the libraries and the organization of materials and services provided. The hypotheses can be stated as follows:

I. *Primary Hypotheses* (those pertaining to the self-reports of faculty members):

H1   Faculty members who are the heavier users of the library do not rely more significantly on the library's collection of government publications than do those who consult the library less frequently (appropriate definitions are provided in Chapter 4).

H2   There is no statistically significant difference in the incidence of use of the library's documents collection between faculty members of institutions that grant the doctorate and those of institutions offering lesser degree programs.

H3   There is no statistically significant difference in the incidence of use of the library's documents collection between faculty members in one discipline and those in any of the other disciplines.

H4   Documents users within any one of the disciplines under study fall into similar areas of teaching specialities.

H5   There is no statistically significant difference among faculty members for limited use or non-use of government publications.

H6   Faculty members in one discipline do not differ significantly from those in any of the other disciplines as to the purposes for which they consult government publications.

H7   (a) Degree offered or discipline are not significant factors in accounting for how often faculty members seek assistance from library staff members; (b) frequency of documents use is not a significant factor in accounting for how often faculty members seek assistance from library staff members.

H8   There is no statistically significant difference between the frequency with which faculty members ask library staff members for assistance and any reluctance on the part of faculty members to request it.

H9   (a) Social scientists do not differ significantly according to discipline or highest degree offered regarding the kinds of assistance that they ask from the library staff; (b) they are not more likely to approach library staff members for assistance in locating a specific document than they are to request reference assistance (that is, aid in finding materials or information to answer a specific question or solve some problem on which they are working).

H10   (a) Social scientists do not differ significantly across disciplines or institutions as to their means of locating needed government publications; (b) for access to government information held in the library, they rely primarily on the public card catalog or citations to documents found in the general literature or special bibliographies of their subject field.

H11   There is no statistically significant difference among faculty members as to how they learned to find materials in the documents collection.

H12   There is no statistically significant difference across discipline, highest degree offered, or institutional control as to the levels of government (Federal, state, and municipal) of which publications are used.

H13   There is no statistically significant difference between faculty members engaged in sponsored research projects and those who are not as to their use of computerized search systems that access government information contained in bibliographic or numeric data bases.

H14   There is no statistically significant difference between the source of funding and whether or not machine-readable data bases are searched.

H15   Social scientists do not differ signficantly across disciplines or highest degree offered as to the specific search system(s) used.

H16   There is no statistically significant difference among faculty members as to which specific indexes are consulted.

H17   Among all of the indexes, faculty members will consult the *Monthly Catalog of United States Government Publications* most frequently.

H18   There is no statistically significant difference among faculty members according to highest degree offered, discipline, institutional control, or frequency of documents use as to the means by which they locate the publications of (a) the United States government, (b) state governments, and (c) municipal governments.

H19   (a) There is no statistically significant difference across discipline or highest degree offered as to the age of the government publications most frequently consulted; (b) the age of the government publications consulted does not vary significantly with the level of government that issued them.

H20   The variables of frequency of library use, discipline, or highest degree offered are not statistically significant factors for determining whether or not a social scientist is currently engaged in, or has completed within the past year, a scholarly activity intended for publication which cited a government publication(s) in the bibliography or footnotes.

H21   A majority of faculty members are unaware of the variety of programs librarians use to promote awareness of government publications.

H22   There is no statistically significant difference across discipline, highest degree offered, institution, or frequency of documents use as to the means by which faculty members make students aware of the government publications collection at the university or college library.

H23   Faculty members, regardless of the extent of their documents use, the method by which they learned to find government publications, discipline, or highest degree offered, do not differ significantly in their preference as to the means by which library staff members instruct students about government publications.

II. *Secondary Hypotheses* (those relating to the library):

H1   The academic library collects, or has access to, the publications from the different levels of government needed and used by its faculty members.

H2   There is a statistically significant relationship between the frequency of faculty use of government publictions and:

(a)   the organization of the government publications collection (government publications in integrated or mixed collections are used more heavily than documents kept in separate collections);

(b)   the classification scheme (use is greater when documents are classified according to widely known schemes such as the Library of Congress or Dewey than when specialized ones such as SUDOC are employed);

(c)   the percentage of depository items received;

(d)   the percentage of government publications entered into the public card catalog;

(e)   the number of staff members employed in the servicing of government publications;

(f)   The circulation of government publications to faculty members;

(g)   1. whether or not the library has a regular program for informing faculty members and students of important government publications (those libraries promoting use have the greatest level of documents use)
       2. faculty members' awareness of the variety of programs offered

H3   Faculty members associated with institutions whose libraries incorporate government publications into the general collection are not more likely to browse for documents than are their counterparts at institutions in which the libraries' documents collections are separate.

SUMMARY OF FINDINGS

The study examined faculty members' self-reports of the following descriptive characteristics in selected academic depository institutions (see Fig. 1-1): (1) general library use in comparison to use of the library documents collection; (2) purpose for documents use; (3) methods for locating needed information in documents; (4) extent and type of assistance received from library staff in their use of documents; (5) reasons for their non-use of documents; and (6) awareness of library promotional programs for documents.

Depositories were analyzed in terms of institutional type (public or private), highest degree offerings, organization of documents collection (separate, integrated, or partially integrated), documents collections other than Federal, library programs to enhance documents awareness, number of personnel servicing the documents collection, entrance of documents into public card catalog, percentage of depository categories received, documents circulated to faculty members, location of collection, and classification scheme (Superintendent of Documents, Library of Congress, etc.).

Faculty patterns for the use or non-use of documents were analyzed by subject department, subject area of teaching, research activities, teaching responsibilities (graduate or undergraduate courses), and percentage of time spent in teaching and research per academic year.

Two data-collection devices were employed in the investigation: questionnaires and interviews. A questionnaire was mailed to the social scientists, and another was sent to the librarians in charge of the documents collections. Interviews served, in part, as a cross-check on certain questionnaire findings, but they also provided additional insights into the reasons for use and non-use of government publications by the social scientists selected.

After pretesting the two questionnaires were mailed to the entire sample in the fall of 1977. Of the 918 faculty questionnaires mailed, 74.4 percent (683) were returned. An examination of the respondents by discipline showed that they comprised 151 economists, 195 historians, 153 political scientists, and 184 sociologists. Chi square analysis indicated that distributions for the first group of respondents did not differ significantly from those responding to each follow-up procedure. The findings, therefore, are representative of the views of heavy, moderate, and limited users, as well as non-users of government publications.[2]

[2] Definitions for these categories will be found in Chapter 4.

General Library Use in Comparison with Use of the Library Documents Collections

In order to place the use of documents collections held by libraries in proper context, social scientists were asked to estimate the frequency of their library use for the previous year. The purpose was to gain a general impression of how often visits to the library involved the use of government publications. On the basis of their responses, social scientists were characterized as heavy, moderate, and limited users, as well as non-users of the library. Data were skewed, in that over three-fourths of the respondents were heavy users; they consulted the library, for a variety of reasons, more than twenty times during the previous year.

Faculty members were also asked to indicate the frequency with which they consulted their institutional libraries' collections of government publications during the same time period. On the basis of their responses, they have been placed into categories of heavy, moderate, and limited users, as well as non-users of documents. Responses were more evenly distributed among categories here than they were for the preceding question. Chi square analysis between frequency of library use and frequency of documents use indicated a statististically significant difference among categories. There were differences, for example, between moderate and limited users of their documents collections. This finding lends support for the adoption of frequency of use as a variable in hypothesis testing.

The return sample was representative of the full-time social scientists surveyed and of the various frequencies of documents use. This is evident from the high return rate for the faculty questionnaire and from the distribution of responses to the time frame in which questionnaires were received. Heavy and moderate documents users were no more likely to respond with reminders than were limited users and non-users. In addition, the nonrespondents to the questionnaire who were interviewed represented heavy, moderate, and limited users, as well as non-users of government publications.

It was found that economists and political scientists accounted for the largest percentage of heavy and moderate users of government publications. Sociologists almost evenly divided among heavy and moderate users, and limited users and non-users; on the other hand, only 40 percent of the historians were heavy or moderate users.

Highest degree offered by the institution was not a statistically significant factor in documents use. Faculty members at baccalaureate and master's-granting institutions are as likely to use government publications as those social scientists situated in doctorate-granting institutions.

Faculty use of government publications was compared with such library variables as collection arrangement, classification scheme, percentage of depository items received, documents entered into public card catalog, and staff size. Statistically significant differences did not result.

9

It should be noted that non-users of government publications may be of the opinion that the levels of government under study publish little or nothing of value to their field. No attempt was made, however, to assess the extent of government publishing in particular social science disciplines, to assess promotional programs, or to alter general faculty awareness and perceptions.

Purposes of Documents Use

When asked about the purposes for which they consult government publications, social scientists were given eight categories of purposes from which to select and were encouraged to check as many options as applied. The Spearman Rank Order Correlation Coefficient showed moderate to strong statistically significant relationships among disciplines.

A major reason for social scientists' use of documents, regardless of discipline, is to obtain census or normative data. Interview subjects also emphasized the value of statistical data, both current and retrospective. They also rely on preliminary reports, advance reports, special studies, and the Public Use Tapes of the Bureau of the Census. Some of the interview subjects indicated on their questionnaires that there is no discernable pattern to the age of government publications consulted. They explain that when they seek retrospective information, it is primarily statistical and produced by the Bureau of the Census. This finding suggests that statistical publications have a longer life span than many other types of government publications; documents librarians should, therefore, expand their collections of statistical publications over time.

Another questionnaire category constituted "current events and issues of interest." Economists rated this option third among the purposes for which they use documents, whereas political scientists listed it first along with census or normative data. Both sociologists and historians listed this category fourth. However, elsewhere in the questionnaire social scientists were asked about the ages of the documents that they consult most often. Except for the historians, they mainly seek current publications produced within the last three years. Economists, political scientists, and sociologists have a wide range of purposes for which they use current publications: they use them for census or normative information, current events and issues of interest, research and technical reports, and resources of value to students.

Methods for Locating Needed
Information in Documents

A comparison of the methods used to locate documents from the levels of government for which publications are sought showed that regardless of discipline, social scientists rely extensively on the monographic, periodical, and bibliograhic literature of their discipline for awareness of what governments issue. Mailing lists constitute the second most frequently mentioned source of references for economists and sociologists seeking current Federal information. These mailing lists allow them to receive not only lists of new publications but in some cases also the publications themselves and ephemera. With these sources of information they can keep abreast of new developments and policy changes. Historians, on the other hand, are the most likely to draw upon librarians for assistance. They rated assistance from library staff members as a third priority technique, whereas the other social scientists listed staff assistance between fifth and eighth in importance as sources of information about newly appearing Federal documents.

As for state publications, economists and political scientists listed citations in the monographic and periodical literature of their disciplines as their most important sources of information, and, second, contacting state agencies. Sociologists reversed that order, while historians listed their subject literature first and assistance from library staff members second. It should be noted that indexes such as the Library of Congress' *Monthly Checklist of State Publications* play a minor role in fulfulling the information requirements of social scientists.

Only 13.8 percent of the respondents use municipal publications at all. Given the small number of responses, it is evident that municipal publications do not constitute an important source of information for many social scientists. Again, indexes are infrequently consulted. Faculty members are more likely to rely on their subject literature and contracting municipal agencies, colleagues, and librarians for information about municipal documents.

At one of the interview sites, faculty members were heavily involved in municipal research and had been recipients of research grants from local government. Since the city in which the academic institution is located had an Urban Observatory, they are able to undertake sponsored research projects which their community wanted. Much of the source material needed for these projects is obtained from the municipal agencies themselves.

Social scientists frequently do not rely on one single method for locating needed government publications or information. It is not uncommon for them to use different methods, depending on such factors as the purpose for which the publications are needed and the recency of the published information. Apparently, many of them do not engage in extensive literature searches to uncover all the potential source material on a given topic. Insead they rely on agencies and sources already familiar to them or confine their searches to a few types of government publications.

Extent and Type of Assistance Received
from Library Staff Members
in the Use of Documents

The chi square test disclosed a statistically significant relationship between frequency of documents use and how often library staff members are asked for assistance. Library users, regardless of the frequency of their documents use, are likely to request assistance only occasionally. Over one-half of the documents users request assistance only sometimes, whereas more than one-fourth need assistance "frequently."

Documents users were asked if they are reluctant to seek assistance in using the government publications collection; only 7.2 percent responded affirmatively. It might be noted that sixteen of these social scientists were associated with two institutions, one of which was an interview site. At this institution, two interview subjects suggested that certain library staff members provide discourteous and incomplete reference service for their students.

One questionnaire item queried social scientists about the kinds of assistance that they request from library staff members. Although not all the categories are mutually exclusive or discrete entities, it was found that social scientists are as likely to request assistance in locating specific documents as they are to request reference assistance (i.e., aid in finding materials or information to answer a specific question or solve some problem on which they are working). Frequency of documents use did not produce a statistically significant difference, and requests for assistance took different forms. These findings underscore the fact that social scientists have diverse needs and interests and that various problems emerge in the search for government publications and information.

Reasons for Non-Use of Documents

Only 16.4 percent of the respondents do not use government publications at all. Some of these social scientists had not been members of their respective departments the previous year, had consulted documents holdings of other libraries, and/or obtained personal copies of needed documents. As these faculty members do not technically constitute non-users, they were deducted from the original percentage. The revised percentage became 13.9.

These social scientists were asked if there are any particular aspects of their libraries' government publications collections and their organization which they feel to be barriers to use or causes of frustration or confusion. Only 12.4 percent of the non-users answered in the affirmative. The most frequently cited reasons are that public card catalogs cover government publications only selectively and that the Superintendent of Documents Classification Scheme is confusing. The small percentage of faculty members responding in the affirmative suggests that the more important, self-reported reasons for non-use are that government bodies publish little or nothing of value to their subject specializations and that too much time is required to gather needed government information. During the interview phase, social scientists elaborated on the time factor, stating that they do not always need government publications for their teaching—that, instead, they rely on current, capsulized information found in newspapers, periodicals, and loose-leaf services. Government publications, some reported, provide in-depth coverage, but it may be too time-consuming to extract the few pieces of pertinent information. Another related problem is that because governments publish so extensively it can be difficult to locate the few publications most beneficial to immediate needs.

Awareness of Library Promotional
Programs for Documents

A majority of faculty respondents are unaware of any documents promotional programs are those who have used them: as support for this assumption, it was know what programs are provided, that their institutional library has no regular program, or that they are guessing about what programs might be available. It might be hypothesized that those most knowledgeable about library "outreach" programs are those who have used them: as support for this assumption, it was found that 80 percent of the social scientists whose students have received classroom instruction have, in fact, invited a librarian to provide formal instruction on the use of the library.

About one-fourth of the respondents have never had occasion to promote the use of the documents collection by their students. Those promoting the collection show a preference for informal methods such as suggesting the collection as a valuable source of information and referring students to the library. As the categories presented in the questionnaire item were not mutually exclusive, and as social scientists could check as many options as were applicable, the chi square test was not performed. It was found that a larger percentage of heavy and moderate users of documents encourage student awareness of the genre by both formal and informal means than do limited users and non-users.

Another questionnaire item asked respondents, both users and non-users, to specify the method of instruction which they prefer the library to undertake for assisting students in using government publications. Half of the social scientists favor instruction through library class lectures or other documents "outreach" programs. Statistical analyses did not disclose significant differences in relation to the variables of frequency of documents use, discipline, the method by which faculty members learn to use the documents collection, the age of documents consulted, and highest degree offered by the instruction.

Interview subjects whose students use government publications related problems encountered by their students in the completion of assignments. They suggested that certain students appear to be overwhelmed by the extent of government publishing, confused by libraries' handling of these publications, and cautious in their dealings with some library staff members. Some social scientists try to minimize these problems by working closely with students in their search for government publications. However, it might be pointed out that most faculty respondents have themselves learned to find materials in the documents collection by informal means, such as trial-and-error processes in using the collection, instruction from library staff members at times of need, and self-instruction. Interview subjects frequently pass on to students those search procedures which they feel the "most comfortable with," even if these methods are "inefficient."

They do not encourage an extensive formal participation by library staff members in making search strategies more systematic.

Documents librarians were asked if their libraries have regular programs for informing faculty members about new acquisitions and services available for government publications. Fourteen libraries had "outreach" programs, but they rely on only a few methods, primarily displays, tours, and library lectures provided for classroom instruction. The present study did not probe the objectives, extent of use, and value of the various methods of documents orientation and instruction; further investigation of the subject is needed.

CONCLUSIONS

It was outside the scope of the investigation to make an intensive examination of the documents collections held by the academic libraries under study and of the different types of publications acquired. However, the information requirements of social scientists, as revealed through the questionnaire and interview responses, have implications for academic documents librarians planning the controlled growth of documents collections and needing to emphasize weeding and selective acquisition in order to avoid congestion in the processing and storage of government publications. Two qualifications might be inserted at this point: (1) The following observations pertain only to full-time social scientists in the disciplines of economics, history, political science, and sociology; and (2) the degree to which these social scientists are typical or atypical of all users of government publications collections located in academic depository libraries merits investigation.

Informed readers will recognize that some of the observations reported here may be equally valid in other segments of library work. The problem of making documents available when needed by library users may be different by an order of magnitude from providing other library materials, given the high rate of obsolescence for many documents and the ephemeral nature of a substantial proportion of the material. Still, collection development for government publications, as well as other library materials, embodies such factors as determining how much material to acquire and in how many copies, how long to retain it, and how to manage what is kept (Buckland, 1975, p. 3).

Social scientists other than historians rely primarily on current publications produced within the past three years. Some of these publications constitute informational matter reflecting current issues, developments, and policy changes, and are available in the form of ephemera which soon superseded by other items. Current ephemera such as public announcements and press releases traditionally have been outside the scope of documents collecting policies for many academic libraries. However, academic librarians might be advised to acquire ephemera selectively and/or to identify which government departments, agencies, and Congressional committees offer such items, in order that their clientele can expand their own contacts for this type of information.

The interviews suggested that social scientists, including historians, regardless of institutional control or degree programs, are drawing upon comparatively few types of publications; those used most are primarily statistical publications, census reports, Congressional hearings and committee prints, annual reports, court cases, certain foreign policy material, serial set items, and reports of investigations conducted by Federal agencies and special commissions. This suggests that documents librarians situated at partial depositories should be able to concentrate on documents collecting policies within these types of publications. It is also conceivable that some of these documents might be collected selectively or not at all by some libraries.

Social scientists other than historians seek retrospective publications primarily for statistical data or census reports. Even the historians interviewed who use government publications rely heavily upon census publications. This finding suggests that academic libraries may find it desirable to expand their collections of statistical data over time at the expense of acquiring certain other types of publications which are used less frequently. Certainly, the area of the selection of government publications merits further investigation. It does seem, however, that current information deserves greater emphasis in the documents collecting policies of academic depository libraries.

The discussion thus far has focused primarily on one aspect of collection building—acquisitions. However, the findings of the investigation have implications for other aspects as well, namely for a systematic retention program and for the dissemination of current information.

As noted in Chapter 4, interview subjects indicated that a subset of titles issued primarily in serial form accounts for a large percentage of their demands on the government publications collection. This finding, which is consistent with Bradford's law of scattering, suggests a principle of diminishing returns with respect to collection building and has implications for the number of titles acquired by depository libraries and for the length of time that these publications are retained.

The reliance of social scientists other than historians on current publications suggest a short life span for many government publications of potential interest to social scientists, especially those which do not constitute one of the types already specified. Ephemera, especially public announcements and press releases, have a particularly short life span. Certain of the faculty members interviewed collect and retain such items themselves for class purposes but discard them after two years. They expect that by that time access to the information will be generally available in more conventional sources which libraries might own.

Partial depositories could concentrate their acquisitions on government publications which are heavily used and put less emphasis on those which are used infrequently or have been unused for years. These depositories need not acquire a majority of the publications disseminated by the Government Printing Office and by other governmental agencies.[3] They would be better advised to concentrate selection and retention on those government publications which receive the greatest amount of use and to rely on regional depositories to provide support in the form of lesser used publications.

Through interlibrary loan services and the dissemination of microfiche copies of government publications, regional depositories could supplement the documents collections of partial depositories. However, as was found during the interviews, reliance on these approaches necessitates that the process of obtaining materials be rapid and that depository libraries undertake a major publicity program to inform their clientele that interlibrary loan privileges *are* available for government publications. More flexible loan periods are needed; heavily used publications should circulate for shorter time periods than infrequently used materials. As is apparent, studies of circulation policies and interlibrary loan practices for government publications are needed in order to determine how well user needs are being accommodated. Such studies would also show the degree to which users are aware of these services.

It appears that academic libraries may not be gathering all the types of government publications needed by social scientists and their students; also, libraries may not be receiving and processing certain publications within a time frame acceptable to social scientists. On the other hand, if libraries are in fact performing these functions, their clientele may be largely unaware of it. Libraries therefore need to publicize their acquisition programs and policies.

Social scientists, in part because of their perceptions about the potential value of library documents collections in meeting their need for current publications and information, seek ways to supplement or bypass their libraries' documents collections. Libraries need to acquire certain publications soon after their public release, disseminate notices that these publications have been acquired, and find ways to supplement traditional indexing sources which operate with time lags unacceptable to social scientists.

Selective dissemination services would enhance librarian and user access to current publications and would reduce delay in the dissemination of announcements and publications by governmental bodies. It would be useful if the government Printing Office (GPO) developed a service patterned after that offered by

---

[3]A systematic effort should be made to determine which of the millions of items distributed annually by the Government Printing Office are really needed. During 1976 over fifteen million free publications were distributed through the depository library program. This included 25,152 individual publication titles and 13,823 bills and resolutions of Congress (Schwartzkopf, 1978, 156).

the National Technical Information Service (NTIS).[4] The purpose of the service would be to make available the numerous publications of GPO soon after their public release or on a prepublication basis. Users would construct and forward special interest profiles directly to the Government Printing Office. As an alternative, depository libraries could compile composite profiles reflecting the diverse needs of their faculty members and submit them to GPO. The libraries would then become redistribution centers, exploiting a major information dissemination center for the benefit of their clientele. At the same time librarians would be monitoring certain of the information requirements of their faculty members.

As a companion to a selective dissemination service, the Government Printing Office might develop weekly newsletters, highlighting high interest publications and providing complete bibliographic citations and abstracts for these publications.[5] Some of the social scientists interviewed advocate current awareness services, but they did interject a cautionary note: the subject areas would have to be broad and reflect interdisciplinary relationships among subject specializations. Social scientists propose that depository libraries subscribe to the service, indicate which items they receive, and circulate copies of the newsletters to them.

An expanded role by Government Printing Office might, as a side benefit, reduce the demands upon members of Congress to fill requests for publications and information. Some interview subjects emphasized their reliance on Congressional representatives because they are unaware of other means of speedy access to certain current publications and information.

Although formalized mailing lists constitute an important source in meeting the information requirements of certain social scientists, it would be too time-consuming for librarians to identify all possible mailing lists or to recommend that every governmental department, agency, or Congressional committee prepare mailing lists. If social scientists rely upon the information sources of a comparatively few agencies and committees, this core list could be identified and acquired.

Many interview subjects volunteered that their information-seeking patterns are neither extensive nor systematic. The project team for the study of the information requirements of English social scientists had a similar finding and hypothesized that:

> It is doubtful if the information-seeking behavior of social science researchers is influenced entirely by the nature of social science research, or the motivation and

---

[4]NTIS, an agency within the Department of Commerce, offers Selected Research in Microfiche (SRIM), which is an automatic biweekly service providing technical reports in microfiche for subject areas selected by users.

[5]The *Weekly Government Abstracts* of the National Technical Information Service might serve as a model.

training of researchers: the formal system may play a large part. Bibliographic tools, for example, could perhaps be made more attractive to use, the subjective "payoff" for users could be increased, and the coverage of the primary literature could be improved and in some cases perhaps made more specific. A comprehensive quantitative description of the social science literature is not available. However, while the tools which the social science researcher has at his disposal may be inadequate, the fact remains that social scientists could, by the use of existing services, cover a good deal more of the references than they do. Where services are very bad (for example, difficult to obtain, time consuming to use, or unpleasant or difficult to use) the practitioner can make a good case for ignoring them, even if the knowledge which he himself regards as desirable suffers as a consequence; but the researcher can make no such case. (*Investigation into Information Requirements of the Social Sciences,* 1971, p. 77).

Some interview subjects in the present study, even faculty members involved in research, assume that limited searching is offset by the eventual coverage of the major government publications in the monographic and periodical literature of their discipline. Apparently this assumption serves as a rationale for inadequate literature search techniques.

In the present investigation certain social scientists professed satisfaction with their present level of access to information, even when the number of sources, government and nongovernment, which they consult is small, or even if more authoritative and complete sources are available. It appears from this study that any services offered by governments and libraries which attempt to appeal to a diverse audience ought to address this concept of perceived need satisfaction and demonstrate that the present level of access to information can be increased without a major expenditure of time and finances. Librarians and government officials could determine which information requirements remain unfulfilled, inadequately fulfilled, or inefficiently fulfilled. Programs designed to increase the information base of social scientists could then take into account factors such as the following: (1) new information ought to be presented—that is, information not presented previously in other sources; (2) ease of access is as important as potential value and perceived quality of government publications; (3) past difficulties encountered in locating government publications affects current search strategies; (4) the purposes for which information is sought vary (faculty members will probably expend greater effort to locate information sources needed for research than they will for items used for teaching); and (5) social scientists may be unaware of how to exploit government publications collections for their own use.

As is believed for other types of publications found in libraries, the possession of government publications by libraries does not guarantee their utilization. Depository libraries, if they want to fulfill their potential, need to be aggressive in their relationship with user groups, be attuned to the needs of their clientele, have collections reflecting these needs, and actively promote the effective use of government publications through a variety of "outreach" programs. Since separate collections and special classification systems, such as that of the Superintendent of Documents, add to the confusion of some users, documents "out-reach" enables libraries to interpret and adjust the formal library structure to meet legitimate needs. In some cases, librarians may find it beneficial to elimi-nate separate collections and specialized classification systems.[6]

That social scientists need instruction in how to search for government publications and information is evidenced by their unsystematic search strate-gies and by the fact that many of them rely on informal means for encouraging student use of documents collections. Some interview subjects also expressed reservations about their own ability to find needed government publications. They pass along to their students whatever methods work best for them, even when they know that these methods are "unsystematic" or "haphazard." As search strategies shaped from years of experience are often difficult to modify, the most opportune time for librarians to affect search strategies would seem to be while individuals are still in graduate school, learning the processes by which needed publications and information can be obtained.

The internal library variables analyzed in Chapter 5 did not disclose statistically significant relationships. This finding indicates that social scientists adjust their library search strategies to accommodate local circumstances and that research designs based solely on factors internal to the library such as col-lection arrangement may be too narrowly conceived. Instead more attention should be given to such institutional characteristics as mission statements, highest degree offered, and curriculum.

The investigation was based on faculty self-reports of their use and non-use of government publications. One limitation to self-reporting is that it may produce systematic bias in certain of the responses and inflate the role of govern-ment publications in meeting the information requirements of social scientists. It could suggest an overestimation of the frequency by which social scientists consult government publications. Interviewing served, in part, as a validation of questionnaire responses and as a check on self-reporting.

It was found that government publications help meet the information requirements of many interview subjects. The faculty members interviewed detailed their search strategies for locating various types of government publica-tions and suggested examples of documents which addressed their teaching and research wants. The major reason for infrequent use and non-use of government publications is that many faculty members believe that governments publish little or nothing of value in their subject specialization. The author recognizes that certain respondents to the questionnaire might have made this response to convey the impression that they are better informed of the extent and type of publishing in their specialization than is actually the case. The limitations of self-reporting have therefore necessitated caution in the interpretation of certain

---

[6]When computer access becomes commonplace, separate collections with separate classification schemes may not hinder access to government publications. It may not matter what the call number is, or where the material is located.

hypotheses. Further investigations of user behavior might adopt methodologies that go beyond self-reporting and involve unobtrusive measures.

From the study reported here it is not possible to state categorically whether or not government publications held by depository libraries are an underutilized source of information. However, it is apparent that libraries constitute only one means by which social scientists gain access to government publications and information, that many social scientists do not exploit those publications to their potential, and that many faculty members limit their use of government publications to a few types and to a small number of titles. If government publications held by libraries are indeed underutilized, it may be due partially to the collection-building policies of the depository libraries themselves. Social scientists interviewed perceive library documents collections as having minimal value in meeting some of their information requirements.

Finally, an observation about use studies is in order. They reflect the conditions, opinions, and search strategies of survey subjects at a particular time. If factors such as variation in promotional techniques and more personalized reference service alter existing use and non-use patterns, the findings may become invalid. Use studies should not be viewed as one-time efforts, but as part of on-going processes intended to better meet the legitimate needs of clientele, present and potential. In this way academic librarians working with depositories of government publications can effectively address the commonly held assumption that government publications comprise an underutilized library resource.

RECOMMENDATIONS FOR FURTHER STUDY

A number of topics emerged during the process of completing the study which merit additional investigation. These include

1. delay time in the dissemination of publications by the Government Printing Office and the handling of publications by depository libraries;
2. development of selective dissemination and current awareness services by the Government Printing Office;
3. circulation policies and interlibrary loan practices for government publications;
4. identification of the core literature of government publications for individual disciplines and across the social sciences.
5. identification of the core agency and legislative mailing lists;
6. given the reliance of social scientists on statistical data, expansion of the *American Statistical Index* by Congressional Information Service to include statistical data published before the decade of the 1960s;
7. types of government publications used by social scientists and of the rate of obsolescence for documents; findings would assist documents librarians in planning the controlled growth of documents collections;

8. use of government publications by faculty members in other disciplines, by faculty members at nondepository institutions, by students, and by members of academic institutions in other countries;
9. user search strategies for locating government publications and information employing research methodologies which do not rely solely on faculty self-reports;
10. the degree to which monographic and periodical literature of a discipline draw together the principal official documents for that field;
11. the delay time involved in publication of the original document and its appearance in monographic and periodical literature;
12. frequency of documents use in relation to internal library variables such as staffing and the organization of the documents collection;
13. components variables in satisfaction of need;
14. reasons for faculty members at doctorate granting institutions not making more statistically significant use of library documents collections than those found at institutions offering lesser degree programs;
15. reasons for the heavy use of the *Index to U.S. Government Periodicals.*

2. Survey of Studies of Document Use

THE FOUR STUDIES OF FEDERAL DOCUMENTS

A search of the literature from 1943 to 1972 made by McCaghy and Purcell "reveals that no study showing use characteristics and needs related to government publications has ever been reported. Most of the literature is concerned with the acquisition, organization, or administration of documents, not with their use" (McCaghy & Purcell, 1972, 7-8). Their survey of patterns of faculty use of documents was made with the expectation that it "might serve as a stimulus for other studies of the users of government publications and as a reference point to which such studies can be compared" (McCaghy & Purcell, 1972, 8). Subsequent studies have patterned their questionnaires upon this study, have investigated use patterns at single institutions, and have concentrated analysis largely on publications of the Federal government. McCaghy and Purcell investigated faculty use of documents at Freiberger Library, Case Western Reserve University, by sampling one-third of the faculty members in the social sciences and humanities. Faculty members in the physical and biological sciences were excluded, as the Library had only a small collection of documents in these disciplines.

A study by Wilson at Trinity University in San Antonio, Texas, surveyed all full-time teaching faculty members and included responses from twenty-three science faculty members (Wilson, 1973, 76-80). Neither study detailed sampling procedures, but total responses were tabulated. The studies did not analyze data separately for social sciences, physical and biological sciences, or humanities, nor by teaching departments. Conclusions from these studies indicate that analysis by total responses results in overly generalized conclusions and does not clarify use and non-use patterns. McCaghy and Purcell concluded that only ten of the 103 faculty members surveyed used the *Monthly Catalog of United States Government Publications*. They did not, however, point out that not all faculty members *need* government publications. Faculty members in history, for example, have varying needs, those in ancient history may not use United States documents for teaching and research, whereas most American historians probably do.

McIlvaine investigated documents use at the University of Connecticut and patterned her questionnaire "loosely" after that of the Case Western University study (McIlvaine, 1975, 49-510). However, direct comparisons of data are not possible due to changes in emphasis and wording reflecting local circumstances. Again only total responses were tabulated. In 1972 the Government Publications Department at the University at Connecticut began issuing to all faculty members a selective monthly list of new acquisitions. A questionnaire was attached to the list for May 1974. The return rate was only 12.3 percent. "No efforts were made to increase the return by further contact" (McIlvaine, 1975, 49). No reason was given for this decision. It would have been beneficial to have queried nonresponding faculty members about their reasons for not participating and to have separated the survey from the acquisition list. Possible reasons for the low return rate may have been that the acquisitions list was not widely consulted and that the survey was undertaken late in the school term when faculty members were preoccupied with other demands on their time. McIlvaine did note that faculty respondents were mainly heavy users of the library regardless of their frequency of documents use. These library users, in her opinion, were more inclined to use government publications in their professional work (McIlvaine, 1975, 51). This finding reinforces the impression that many faculty members may not have consulted the library acquisitions list.

Hernon and Williams (1976, 93-108) surveyed full-time faculty members at the University of Nebraska at Omaha regarding their use and non-use of United States government publications. Questionnaire data were tabulated by total response; by broad groupings, such as the social sciences, humanities, physical and biological sciences; and by individual departments. Selected interviews were employed for history, psychology, social welfare, English, music, physics, and engineering and technology. Interview subjects were selected on the basis of known research and teaching interests. It was not specified if interview subjects comprised both those returning and those not returning questionnaires; most subjects, in fact, had returned questionnaires.

The earlier studies had employed only the questionnaire technique. Interviewing, Hernon and Williams felt, was necessary to clarify certain questionnaire responses. For example, interviews indicated that faculty members considered the integrating of instruction in the use of government documents into the subject courses a better method of accomplishing this goal than using an independent course.

The other studies had better return rates than McIlvaine's (12.3 percent—120 out of 975 full-time faculty). Of the 116 faculty members randomly selected by McCaghy and Purcell, 103, or 89 percent, completed and returned questionnaires. Wilson distributed 171 questionnaires and had 100 (58 percent) returned, whereas Hernon and Williams obtained a 51 percent response (450 faculty surveyed) after employing a follow-up questionnaire. They also had a 50 percent response per department.

The McCaghy and Purcell study revealed a significant rate of non-use (62 percent) for the library's documents collection, whereas Wilson found that only 32 percent of the respondents made no use at all of Federal documents. For Hernon and Williams, this percentage was 31. The difference may be accounted for by the fact that McCaghy and Purcell included faculty members who used other libraries and who obtained personal copies of government publications in this total. They also sampled faculty members randomly and excluded science faculty members, while including those in the humanities. Faculty use and non-use of government publications must be judged in relation to their utilization of other library resources and to the efforts of campus librarians to promote usage of library resources.

The difference in percentage of documents non-use may suggest that non-respondents are, in fact, non-users. On the other hand, the difference may be accounted for by the divergence in response rates, which ranged from 12.3 to 89 percent. A distinction must be made between non-users of the library's documents collection and non-users of government publications. Some faculty members use documents held by other libraries, or they own personal copies of documents. As only the McCaghy and Purcell study reported this distinction, comparisons among the studies are further impaired.[1]

The reported studies cannot accurately reveal general documents use, since each concerns faculty use on *one* campus. Extensive comparisons among these campuses are difficult given the differences in sampling procedures and questionnaire emphasis. Each questionnaire was modified to meet local needs, and there is no indication that any of the questionnaires were pretested. A weakness of all of the studies is that data were analyzed only by percentages. More powerful statistical analyses were not employed for hypothesis testing.

RELATED STUDIES

The Government Publications Department at the Northwestern University Library investigated the use of certain documents, primarily those of the United Nations, for the period 1968 through 1972 (Danielson, 1973, 14-146). The

---

[1]The present study asked infrequent users and non-users of government publications if they consulted documents collections located in other libraries or if they owned personal copies of documents. The findings are presented in Chapter 4.

study was based on a count of those documents charged for use outside the library. In order to compare these statistics to their estimates of use, to gather information concerning the value of United Nations publications, and to stimulate an awareness of the existence of the collection, the library staff placed an eight-item questionnaire in the mail boxes of 261 faculty members and student assistants in the departments of economics, education, geography, history, political science, sociology, and in the Graduate School of Management. An additional 460 questionnaires were left at three entrances fo the library. However, there were only thirty-six returns, twenty-two of which were from faculty members. The low response rate underscores the need for follow-up procedures, for stressing the value of the survey even to those persons who may be regular documents users, and for supplementing questionnaires with other data-collecting devices. According to the author, some of the questionnaires went unnoticed in the mail boxes.

In 1956 DeVelbiss examined how academic library users at the University of California approached the Federal government publications they borrowed (DeVelbiss, 1956). She found that approximately 60 percent of the publications which circulated during the time of her investigation were located through the subject card catalog. However, many libraries enter only a small percentage of their documents holdings into the public card catalog.

Both the Northwestern University and DeVelbiss studies offer different methodologies for the study of documents use. However, many libraries would be unable to duplicate such studies because they do not retain circulation records for documents, nor do they follow similar record-keeping practices. Such studies have an additional weakness in that they do not account for use within the library.

Two other studies merit mention, although they do not cover the publications of the various levels of government under investigation here. In a national survey of Canadian Federal and provincial government publications, Edith Jarvi (1976, p. 38) conducted interviews at selected academic libraries in her country and found that "about half of the library users interviewed [faculty members comprised only a few of these] . . . were not aware that separate document collections exist." She also noted that "too many reported experiencing great frustration in using the collection." Of particular importance to the investigation reported here is the finding that the faculties requiring documents use "most frequently, were, in the following order, economics, political science, history, and sociology" (Jarvi, 1976, p. 39). These are the same departments which this study had examined. The Canadian study contains methodological weaknesses which its author admits. However, it does underscore the fact that concern with documents utilization is not confined to librarians within the United States.

A comprehensive survey of social scientists was conducted in the United Kingdom between 1967 and 1970 (*Investigation into Information Requirements of the Social Sciences,* 1971). The project staff members included government publications as one of the physical forms of information. However, they did not specify different levels of government, engage in hypothesis testing, or include formal departments of history. They presented their data largely in a descriptive manner so that the reader could supply interpretation. Also their selection of data categorizations were not similar to those of the documents use studies previously mentioned.

In summary, it is difficult to compare past documents use studies due to differences in methodologies, return rates, modifications in survey instruments, and variations in data categorizations and analyses of findings. Future studies need to consider the publications of all levels of government (Weech, 1978, 177-184).

3. Research Methodology

OVERVIEW OF THE DEPOSITORIES
IN THE STATES STUDIED

The study investigated academic depository libraries in the states of Illinois, Indiana, Michigan, and Ohio. Table 3-1, which relates the number of depositories to the states having the largest populations, suggests that a study of depository libraries in these four states should have value beyond the geographic area. Both columns are quite similar, the only major difference being that Massachusetts has fewer than thirty depositories, whereas Virginia ranks fourteenth in population. Indiana is eleventh in population and twelfth in number of depositories, whereas Michigan ranks seventh on both lists, and Ohio in sixth in population and fifth in number of depositories.

Within the four states, there are 172 depository libraries, of which ninety-seven are located in academic institutions, private and public, with degree programs ranging from the baccalaureate to the doctorate. Of the thirty depositories in the state of Indiana, nineteen are academic and fall into the sphere of this examination. Excluded are the public libraries, the State Library, special and law libraries, and Indiana University-Purdue University at Fort Wayne (atypical because its governance is divided between two institutions). Illinois has forty-six depositories, of which twenty-eight are appropriate to this study. Those excluded are public libraries, law and special libraries, the State Library, and community colleges. Michigan has forty-five depositories, of which seventeen are associated with academic institutions offering at least the baccalaureate degree.

27

Excluded are special, law, public and county, community college libraries, and the State Library. In Ohio, there are thirty-three academic depositories (out of a total of fifty-one libraries); excluded are public libraries, the Cleveland Municipal Reference Library, the State Library, the Supreme Court Law Library, and community college depositories.

Table 3-1   Ranking of States with Largest Populations and Number of Depository Libraries

Population[1,3]	Depositories[2]
California	California, 96
New York	New York, 72
Pennsylvania	Texas, 56
Texas	Pennsylvania, 53
Illinois	Ohio, 51
Ohio	Illinois, 46
Michigan	Michigan, 45
New Jersey	New Jersey, 36
Florida	Florida, 33
Massachusetts	North Carolina, 32
Indiana	Virginia, 31
North Carolina	Indiana, 30

[1] Based on 1970 Census ranking in *Information Please Almanac, 1975* (New York: Simon and Schuster, 1974), p. 699. The same ranking may also be found in U.S. Dept. of Commerce, Social and Economic Statistics Administration. *Statistical Abstract of the United States 1973* (Washington: GPO, 1973), p. 13.

[2] Based on counting depositories listed in "List of Depository Libraries as of September 1, 1975," *Monthly Catalog of U.S. Government Publications,* September 1975, pp. 167-193.

[3] Population estimates for 1974 indicate a slight shifting in positions for the twelve states. The following order is given: California, New York, Texas, Pennsylvania, Illinois, Ohio, Michigan, Florida, New Jersey, Massachusetts, North Carolina, and Indiana. Indiana, therefore, is twelfth in estimated population and number of depository libraries. U.S. Dept. of Commerce, Bureau of the Census. *Statistical Abstract of the United States 1975* (Washington: GPO 1975), p. 12.

In Indiana, 63 percent, or nineteen of the thirty depository libraries, are academic.[1] This percentage approximates the national average and includes public and private institutions and colleges and universities. Institutional types and degree levels, however, are not uniformly represented. Indiana has no public, but five private, master's-level institutions and has only one private doctorate-granting institution. Unlike Indiana, many states do not have regional campus systems. States such as Illinois, Michigan, and Ohio have community college depositories; Indiana has none. This study does not deal with institutions offering less than four-year programs.

In Illinois, 61 percent, or twenty-eight of the forty-six depository libraries, are academic.[2] Sixty-five percent of Ohio's depository institutions (33 out of 51) are academic. In Michigan, approximately 38 percent, or seventeen of the depository libraries, are associated with academic institutions offering the minimum of the baccalaureate degree. In addition, there are two academic law libraries and eight community college libraries.

Libraries designated as regional depositories are required to receive one copy of all documents available for distribution from the Government Printing Office. By early 1978, there were fifty-one of these libraries. Not all of the states have the one or two regional depositories permitted by law. Regional depositories vary in type from university to public, state, and special libraries, with 57 percent of the regional depositories being academic libraries. Indiana, Illinois, and Ohio have one regional depository each—the State Libraries—but these are excluded from this study since they are not academic depositories. In Michigan, the two regional depositories are the Detroit Public Library and the State Library.

Selection of Institutions, Departments, and Faculty

The academic depository libraries for the four states ("List of Depository Libraries as of September 1, 1975," 1975) were grouped according to institutional control (private and public) and then by highest degree offering (baccalaureate, master's, and doctorate). These classifications were based on the data presented in *Education Directory, 1974-75: Higher Education* (1975).

The departments of economics, history, political science, and sociology were chosen from among those in the social sciences. Therefore it was next determined which of the institutions in the six cells provided courses in these disciplines as part of their highest degree offerings. On the basis of this informa-

[1] For the purposes of this count, Indiana University Law Library and Indiana University-Purdue University at Fort Wayne have been excluded.

[2] Law libraries associated with the University of Illinois and University of Chicago have been excluded from the institutional sampling.

tion, the insitutions depicted in Table 3-2 were selected for investigation during the 1977-78 academic year.[3]

In summary, depository institutions comprise the primary sampling unit. Specific departments representing the social sciences were chosen, and all full-time faculty members within these specified departments were surveyed. Selection of these faculty members enabled the investigator to make a detailed analysis of social scientists and their use and non-use of government publications for current and retrospective information. Hopefully, at the same time, a clear picture of the actual condition of library documents services for these departments emerges.

Data Collecting Instruments

Two research methodologies were employed in the investigation: questionnaires and interviews. Questionnaires enabled the investigator to determine and de-

Table 3-2   Seventeen Academic Depository Institutions Surveyed

Type of Institution	Degree Level			Row Totals
	Baccalaureate	Master's	Doctorate	
Private	Hanover College	Butler University	Case Western Reserve University	
	Ohio Wesleyan University	John Carroll University	Northwestern University	
	Principia College	Valparaiso University	Notre Dame University	
	(3)	(3)	(3)	9
Public	Indiana State University, Evansville	Central Michigan University	Indiana University, Bloomington	
	Indiana University, Kokomo	Eastern Illinois University	Michigan State University	
		Western Illinois University	Southern Illinois University, Carbondale	
	(2)	(3)	(3)	8
Column totals	5	6	6	17

[3] See Appendix A for a more complete explanation of the sample selection.

scribe the reasons for faculty use or non-use of government publications by ascertaining a wide range of responses.

In addition to the questionnaires sent to faculty, another questionnaire was mailed to the librarian in charge of the documents collection at each institution to ascertain data about that school and the staffing, organization, classification, acquisition, circulation, servicing, and promotion of government publications. These data provide additional information necessary to understand faculty responses.

Had questionnaires alone been relied upon, they might have produced a self-selected sample in which documents users were more likely to respond than non-users. Therefore interviewing was also used to serve as a precaution against self-selection, as a means for determining if nonrespondents were non-users, as a validation of questionnaire findings, and as a means for obtaining additional explanatory information as to the reasons for use and non-use. Interviewing may also have served as an indication of possible bias in the questionnaire, although, hopefully, pretest procedures minimized bias.

Faculty members at a subsample of institutions (six—one from each of the cells depicted in Table 3-2) were selected for interviewing. Interview subjects, comprising faculty members both returning and not returning questionnaires, were chosen after questionnaire data were analyzed. Interview questions were, therefore, formulated partly on the basis of questionnaire responses. The investigator wanted to determine beforehand whether each institution in a particular cell was similar or whether one diverged widely from the others. Faculty members at "maverick" institutions were selected for interviews in an effort to determine why they exhibited use patterns different from their counterparts at institutions having similar control and highest degree offered.[4]

LIMITATIONS

Certain limitations arise with a survey of this type, but hopefully their impact can be minimized. Since not all of the institutions in the population could be surveyed, stratified random sampling procedures were used. Unfortunately for one category, private master's-level institutions, the author could not include three schools offering graduate degrees in all four disciplines. However, as the study included academic depositories from four of the more populous states, it is reflective of the programs offered by institutions in this category.

The author was aware that he was describing reasons for use or non-use and not evaluating or assessing utilization patterns. He also tried to guard against personal biases and preconceptions about the quality of information contained in government publications and against creating the impression that if materials *were* available they *would* be used. The objective was to ascertain reasons for use

[4]See Appendix B for a discussion of interviewing.

or non-use and not to alter utilization patterns, although presumably a clearer understanding of such factors could lead to enhancement of documents utilization in libraries.

A minimal return rate might have signified a lack of faculty use of government publications or concern about the survey subject. As a precaution against a low response rate, follow-up procedures were employed. Perhaps people do not return questionnaires for which they can only supply negative answers or no comments. Based on this assumption, the faculty questionnaire began with some closed-ended questions about the individual faculty member's teaching and research interests. The questionnaire, although eight pages in length, was designed so that there were few open-ended questions and so that faculty needed only to check appropriate responses. It was also professionally printed on the assumption that appearance affects the return rate.

Weaknesses may have existed in the faculty questionnaire and interviews themselves. Faculty may have been influenced by the length and wording of the questionnaire, by whether they understood the questions, and by trying to anticipate what the researcher expected. Conversely, they might have answered questions in a negative manner if, for example, they were recently restricted or penalized by a library policy. To minimize such difficulties, the faculty questionnaire was pretested[5] and was found to be satisfactory.

[5] Appendix C explains the pretest procedure.

4. Faculty Study Results

This chapter examines the hypotheses generated from those descriptive characteristics (general library use in comparison to library documents use, purpose for documents use, method for locating needed information, extent and type of assistance received from library staff, reasons for non-use, and awareness of library promotional programs for documents) depicted in Chapter 1. In general, these hypotheses are analyzed primarily in terms of the following variables: institutional control, highest degree offering, subject discipline, and frequency of documents use.

For the purpose of analysis, the Statistical Package for the Social Sciences (SPSS) was used. Descriptive data were grouped by frequency distributions and percentages and displayed in tabular and graph format. The data included in the analyses of relationships between variables were presented in the form of contingency tables. The chi square test was used to test for significance of relationships between the two variables being investigated in each relationship. Because the disciplines under study comprise a subset of their institutions, data were also arranged so as to reflect this "nested" design.[1] By collapsing data, the chi square test of statistical significance could then be employed. The Spearman Rank Order Correlation Coefficient was used for a comparison of rankings among the disciplines of economics, history, political science, and sociology. This measure of association requires that the data be ranked in order of magnitude. For the purposes of testing the significance of relationships between variables, the level

[1] A factor is nested within another factor if each level of the first one appears within the second factor. (For additional information on the concept of nesting see Glass & Stanley, 1970, p. 473.)

of significance was set at 0.05. Nonstatistically significant relationships were also identified, and certain ones are presented in the body of the text.

The results of the analysis of the data collected are given in two main sections. The first of these reports background and general characteristics of the responding faculty, including an examination of their frequency of library and documents use. The second section analyzes faculty questionnaires and interviews in relation to the specific hypotheses stated in Chapter 1 and concludes with a brief report on validity and reliability. For limited users and non-users of government publications, the chapter amplifies the reasons for infrequent use or non-use and describes their methods for locating needed source material.

GENERAL CHARACTERISTICS OF RESPONDING FACULTY

The method of attacking the general descriptive characteristics and the more specific hypotheses utilized a mail questionnaire[2] which was distributed to 918 faculty members. A total of 683, or 74.4 percent, of those polled responded. Of these, 446 faculty members, or 65.3 percent, represented public institutions while 237 faculty members, or 34.7 percent, came from private institutions.[3]

Chi square analysis for the respondents in Table 4-1 shows that distributions by discipline, highest degree offering, and institutional type are significantly different $(\chi^2 (3,5) = 4.914, p < .05)$. Although each grouping according to institutional type and highest degree offered is not proportional, the participation of faculty at baccalaureate institutions is sufficient for the purposes of statistical analysis. However, it may be useful to intrude with a methodological note. The author realizes that a relatively small number of responses to specific questions by faculty members at baccalaureate institutions influences the results of a test for significance of relationships between variables and that a small sample provides an overestimation of the true value. In such cases the data are examined in terms of percentages and collapsed to permit statistical analysis.

Estimation of Time Spent in Professorial Activities

In order to gain an understanding of how faculty members spend their working time, the first questionnaire item asked them to estimate the percentage of their time associated with teaching, research or scholarly writing, administrative duties, and "other" responsibilities. In the "other" category they placed activities such as committee and editorial responsibilities and student advising. Figure 4-1 comprises a histogram based on the estimated percentages for schools having similar institutional control and degree programs. It shows that research or

---

[2] Appendix D contains the faculty questionnaire.

[3] Appendix F analyzes faculty respondents by institution and department.

Table 4-1 Analysis of Responding Disciplines According to
Highest Degree Offering and Institutional Control

	B.A.		M.A.		Ph.D.		
	Private	Public	Private	Public	Private	Public	Row
Discipline	No.[1]	No.	No.	No.	No.	No.	Totals
Economics	7(11)	4(4)	13(19)	32(42)	38(56)	57(75)	151(207)
History	10(12)	5(7)	16(21)	47(59)	40(54)	77(103)	195(256)
Political Science	8(9)	5(5)	10(12)	31(47)	36(54)	63(88)	153(215)
Sociology	6(11)	6(6)	17(18)	46(65)	36(51)	73(89)	184(240)
Totals	31(43)	20(22)	56(70)	156(213)	150(215)	270(355)	683(918)

[1] Numbers in parentheses refer to the full-time faculty members for that particular grouping.

scholarly writing is not confined to institutions offering graduate-level programs,
that the largest percentages of faculty time spent in research are at doctorate-
granting schools, that the percentages for administrative duties across institutional
control and degree programs are similar, and that social scientists at doctorate-
granting institutions spend a lesser proportion of their time teaching than do
their counterparts in institutions having lower degree programs.

The exact percentages reported in Figure 4-1 are as follows:

	Teaching	Research or scholarly writing	Administrative duties	Other
Public baccalaureate institutions	71.6%	19.8%	7.8%	0.8%
Public master's-level institutions	63.3	22.7	12.2	2.0
Public doctorate-granting institutions	42.8	44.4	12.4	2.8
Private baccaluareate institutions	68.7	19.5	8.7	2.6
Private master's-level institutions	66.1	18.5	12.7	2.6
Private doctorate-granting institutions	51.8	34.6	12.2	2.3
Average	60.7	26.6	11.0	2.2

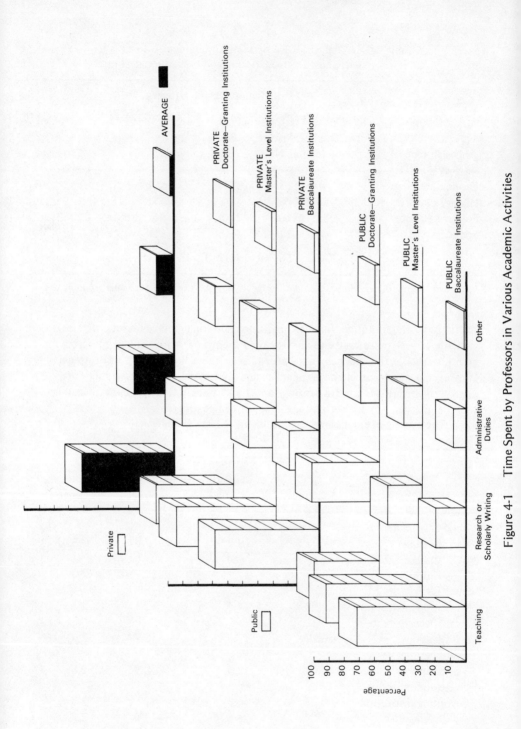

Figure 4-1   Time Spent by Professors in Various Academic Activities

Teaching Responsibilities

The next questionnaire item asked faculty members if the courses which they teach are primarily at the freshman and sophomore level, junior and senior level, graduate (master's) level, or graduate (doctorate) level. It had been hoped that responses here would permit grouping so that the hypotheses could be examined on the basis of teaching levels (undergraduate versus graduate courses, freshman and sophomore versus junior and senior courses, and master's versus doctorate courses). However as respondents often checked more than one level, clear distinctions and patterns among levels did *not* emerge. It should be noted that the variable of highest degree offering permitted comparison of baccalaureate to graduate level programs but could not distinguish within graduate level institutions between those faculty members teaching only undergraduate or graduate level courses. Teaching at graduate institutions is often not confined to one level. Because of this, teaching levels are not reported, except for the comment that responses were representative of all of the teaching levels and combinations. Only thirty-one of the respondents do not teach regularly; these social scientists occupy administrative positions.

Involvement in Research

As faculty involvement in research might be a factor in documents use, one questionnaire item queried social scientists as to whether or not they were currently engaged in, or had recently completed (within the past three years), a research project, either sponsored or nonsponsored. A sponsored project was defined as one having direct financial support from either the institution itself or an external source, such as a governmental agency or private foundation or organization. A total of 358, or 52.4 percent, of the social scientists stated that they had been associated with sponsored projects, while 448, or 65.6 percent, of the faculty had been involved with nonsponsored projects.

Faculty members engaged in sponsored research were asked to identify the source of funding and were encouraged to mark more than one category if applicable. Analysis of the data revealed that the major sources are the institution itself (174), the Federal government (167), and private foundations and organizations (98). Limited use is made of state governments (26), industry or business (17), and local government (5). The use of local government sponsorship was confined to one institution, the University of Notre Dame, and there primarily within the Department of Government and International Studies.

In an attempt to identify trends, the data were collapsed so as to reflect highest degree offerings and the type of funding (governmental, industry or business, private foundations and organizations, and the institution itself). At least some faculty members from all the departments except seven had been recipients of funding. Social scientists at doctorate-granting institutions had

37

received more financial support than faculty members at institutions with lower degree programs. It is interesting that social scientists at private master's-level institutions had received fewer grants than their counterparts at public institutions.

Regardless of highest degree offerings, faculty members rely most extensively on institutional support for their research. Those in public baccalaureate institutions have more governmental than institutional support, while the reverse is found at private baccalaureate institutions. Governmental support at private baccalaureate institutions is confined to the disciplines of economics and sociology.

Use of the Library

In order to place faculty utilization of the library's documents collection into proper context, the social scientists were asked to estimate the number of times that they used the resources of the college or university library during the previous year. For purposes of the testing of hypotheses and statistical analysis, respondents were grouped as heavy, moderate, and limited users, as well as non-users of the library. As the questionnaire had six fixed categories specifying frequencies of use ranging from zero to more than twenty, the assignment of respondents to a grouping was based on response distribution. Most of the respondents (530, or 77.6 percent) went to the library, for whatever reason(s), more than twenty times and therefore comprised the heavy users.[4] The seven faculty members who admitted that they did not need the library at all became the non-users. Although they were not asked to specify their reasons for non-use, three of them stated that they had not been members of the faculty the preceding year. Limited users consulted the library one to five times, while moderate users (120) had used the library between six and twenty times during the previous year.

Use of Government Publications

Respondents were also classified as heavy, moderate, and limited, as well as non-users of the government publications located in their college or university library. The assignment of faculty to each grouping was also based on the distribution of their estimated use of the documents collection. As faculty members using the collection fewer than six times per year were queried further as to the reasons for their infrequent use, non-users became those faculty who did not use the collection at all, and limited users were those social scientists consulting the collection one to five times. Differentiation of the groups of heavy and moderate users was based on the distribution of responses to four categories

---

[4]If the author had been able to foresee such a large percentage of heavy users, the categories would have been altered to permit a wider spread of responses.

ranging from six to more than twenty times. Approximately 385, or 56.4 percent, of the respondents fell into this range. As the midpoint for this range encompassed the category of sixteen to twenty times, heavy users were defined as those faculty using the collection *at least* sixteen times. Moderate users consulted the collection from six to fifteen times.

Before settling on this grouping of library and documents use, the investigator collapsed the data into various combinations and applied the chi square test. Data were obviously skewed by the number of faculty members whose library use had to be labeled as heavy. Still, the results of the chi square test for the data collapsed from Table 4-2 indicated a statistically significant difference among faculty members whose library use was heavy, moderate, or limited, and those whose documents use was heavy, moderate, or limited (x^2 (2,2) = 82.19, $p > .001$). This finding adds support to the particular groupings employed for heavy, moderate, and limited users, as well as non-users of the library and documents collection. As is apparent, distinctions between heavy and moderate use may, in some cases, be arbitrary. Because of this, data analysis will also incorporate heavy and moderate users into one grouping and compare this group to limited users and non-users.

Analysis of the data in Table 4-2 indicates that heavy library users account for 66.5 percent of the documents use; 49.2 percent of their documents use is either moderate or heavy. Some 95.7 percent of the heavy documents users are also heavy library users. It might be useful to repeat that frequencies of library and documents use are based on faculty estimates. Some of the limited documents users consult government publications more than the one to five times. They either have secretaries or student or research assistants who gather needed information or consult the resources of other libraries.

Chi square analysis indicates a statistically significant difference between discipline and frequency of documents use (x^2 (3,3) = 73.65, $p > .001$). Economists account for the largest percentage of heavy and moderate documents use. A total of 72. 9 percent of them are either heavy or moderate users, whereas

Table 4-2   Comparison of the Frequency of Library
and Documents Use

| Frequency of Library Use | Frequency of Documents Use | | | | Total |
	Heavy Number	Moderate Number	Limited Number	Non-Use Number	
Heavy	222	114	118	73	527
Moderate	10	39	52	21	122
Limited	—	—	16	11	27
Non-Use	—	—	—	7	7
Total	232	153	186	112	683

the percentage for political scientists is 63.2 and for sociologists, 54.8. Sociologists are almost evenly split among heavy and moderate users and limited users and non-users. However, with the inclusion of limited users (34 percent), the percentage for sociologists became 88.8. Historians, on the other hand, are predominantly limited users or non-users (60.2 percent).

The frequency of use for the documents collections located in college or university libraries was examined from another perspective. Each questionnaire was coded so that there would be a record of respondents and nonrespondents. Questionnaires for those responding without follow-up reminders were compared to those receiving postcards (two weeks after initial questionnaire distribution, each faculty member was sent a postcard reminder asking for his support and informing him to contact the investigator if questionnaires had been misplaced), second questionnaires, and handwritten letters (to further increase the response among baccalaureate institutions, their nonresponding faculty were sent handwritten letters toward the end of the data collecting phase, asking for their cooperation) in order to determine if there were a statistically significant difference among subgroups as to the frequency of documents use. Some 425, or 62.2 percent, of the respondents returned questionnaires without the necessity of any further intervention. The postcard reminder appealed to 107, or 15.7 percent, and the follow-up questionnaire attracted another 146, or 21.4 percent. The assumption that more frequent users were more likely to participate without any reminder was disproved, as there was no significant difference between subgroups as to the frequency of documents use $(\chi^2 (3,5) = 12.25, p < .05)$. As many non-users and limited users participated without a reminder as did the more frequent users. With each intervention, non-users replied as frequently as users did. This finding suggests that the return sample was representative of those full-time faculty members surveyed.

Reasons for Limited Use
and Non-Use of Government Publications

A total of 298, or 43.6 percent, of the respondents consulted the government publications collections of their college or university library five or fewer times last year. In fact, 112 of these same faculty members did not use the collection at all.

One questionnaire item queried limited users and non-users as to the reason(s) for their infrequent use of documents. The overwhelming response (160) was that governments publish little or nothing of value in their immediate field. The next three most frequently checked categories were that faculty obtain personal copies of needed government publications (79), that the amount of time expended in trying to find relevant information in government publications is out of proportion to what is found (69), and that faculty are unfamiliar with the arrangement of the documents collection (43). A minority of faculty members explained that they are unaware of the existence of such material at the library (31); that they rely on secretaries, students, or research assistants to gather needed government publications (24); and that they consult documents located in a library other than the one on their campus (12). The "other" category attracted twenty-two responses; these focused on the claims that documents are not needed for research and teaching, that faculty consult documents held within the department (for example, those of their colleagues), and that administrative responsibilities are too time-consuming to permit extensive searches for information.

Some of the miscellaneous comments are of interest. One social scientist prefers to consult commercially produced loose-leaf services because they provide information much faster than does the government. Two other faculty members labeled library policies as inhibiting factors by emphasizing lending restrictions and the fact that the documents section of the library is closed at the times (nights, weekends, and holidays) when they prefer to use the collection. A historian relies on Air Force news clips that the African Studies Program receives every two weeks from the State Department; other than for utilizing these clips, he is an infrequent user of documents. It might be noted that only one social scientist admitted that he seldom notices the publisher of material. The other respondents either did not make this distinction or failed to admit it.

Faculty members who checked that they use documents located in their departments or other libraries, obtain personal copies of documents, or rely on support staff to gather needed governmental information, are, in fact, more extensive users of government information than the question pertaining to the frequency of documents use revealed. These social scientists use government publications, but not always those located in the college or university libraries. Therefore, the reasons for limited use and non-use were reexamined but with the exclusion from consideration of those faculty members who marked one or more of these three special reasons. Also excluded were social scientists who were not members of the faculty the preceding year.

Table 4-3 indicates that an overwhelming number of faculty members responded that they believe that governmental agencies publish little or nothing of value to their immediate field. Of the remaining categories, the most frequently checked responses were that the information is out of proportion to the time expended, that faculty are unfamiliar with the arrangement of the collection, and that they are unaware of the existence of such materials at the library.

Comparison of the reasons to the disciplines indicated that historians, regardless of institutional control and highest degree offering, are the most likely to report that governments publish little or nothing of value in their immediate field. To test an assumption that those historians who feel this way are teaching primarily in areas other than American history, limited user and

Table 4-3 Comparison of Disciplines with Reasons for Infrequent Use

Reasons for Infrequent Use	Discipline				
	Economics	History	Political Science	Sociology	Total
Governments publish little or nothing of value in the field	12	80	19	27	138
Unaware of the existence of such materials at the library	3	10	2	10	25
Unfamiliar with arrangement of the government publications collection	3	10	3	12	28
The amount of time expended in trying to find relevant information in government publications is out of proportion to what is found	4	17	14	13	48
The library staff members provide minimal assistance in use of government publications	2	2	2	2	8
Mircoformed government publications are separated from the rest of the government documents collection	1	1	0	0	2
Other	1	5	4	8	18

non-user categories were collapsed into that representing those whose teaching responsibilities relate to the United States and those whose do not. Thirty percent of these historians teach American history, which indicates that the immediate teaching and research interests are more important than the broader field.

The data on limited users and non-users were also examined to determine if faculty in doctorate-granting institutions differ from those in institutions with lower degree programs as to their reasons for infrequent use. Chi square analysis was not performed due to the clustering of responses into a few of the categories and to the number of empty cells. Still, the overwhelming opinion, regardless of highest degree offering and institutional control, is that governments publish little or nothing of value in a particular field. Some support was given to the view that the amount of time expended in trying to find relevant information in government publications is out of proportion to what was found. Social scientists responding to the categories of unfamiliarity with the arrangement of the documents collection and of unawareness of the existence of this collection at the library clustered in doctorate and master's-granting institutions, both public and private. Only two social scientists at baccalaureate institutions marked either response.

In order to obtain additional insights into the reasons for not making use of government publications, non-users were asked if there were any particular aspects of the library's government publications collection and its organization which they felt to be a barrier to utilization or a cause of frustration or confusion. Only 12.4 percent of the non-users answered in the affirmative. These respondents were evenly distributed as to discipline, institutional control, and highest degree offering.

Non-users did emphasize the fact that the public card catalog does not list all of the publications, that the classification scheme is confusing, that there is difficulty in determining which publications the library does or does not have, and that the library does not publish guides explaining the collection. A sociologist wrote that he could not figure out the Superintendent of Documents Classification Scheme "at least not without spending more time than he presently had available." A political scientist noted that his past experiences had shown him that "there was a mass of pertinent material in documents, but no systematic way of determining what was there. I always had the feeling the data I needed was somewhere but who knows where."

However, as is evident from the small percentage of faculty who experienced confusion and frustration, the above-mentioned factors are not generally perceived as major barriers to use. Apparently the more important criteria are their perceptions as to whether government agencies publish in a particular area and the amount of time expended in gathering needed governmental information.

Although documents users were instructed not to complete the question pertaining to frustrating and confusing aspects of the collection and its organization, eighty, or 14 percent, of them wanted their viewpoint known. These social scientists were evenly distributed among the groupings of heavy, moderate, and limited users. The major problems, they felt, are that the classification scheme is confusing (54) and that the public card catalog does not reflect all the government publications held (41). Less frequently mentioned responses were that it is difficult to determine which documents the library does or does not hold (36), needed documents are not on the shelves (25), and the library holds few of the documents needed (18). One limited user from a doctorate-granting institution noted that "the sheer volume" of government publications held by his library was "intimidating; I know of specific sources to meet some of my needs, but am no doubt missing valuable items." Another limited user commented that he relies on the card catalog, mainly the section for authors, for locating needed library information. He felt that "too few government publications have a listed chief author, under whose name the item is listed in the author card catalog, which is by far the most convenient to use." It should be noted that very few of the documents users and non-users indicated that library staff are discourteous, provide unsatisfactory service, appear ill-informed, or seem too busy to have time to deal with their questions.

TESTING THE HYPOTHESES

The remainder of this chapter focuses on the specific faculty hypotheses detailed in Chapter 1. Because of the exploratory nature of this study, the objective behind these hypotheses was to examine findings across institutional control, highest degree offering, discipline, and frequency of documents use. In order to compare institutions, patterns and exceptions are reported among institutions having similar characteristics, control (public or private affiliation), and highest degree offering. In addition, overall frequency distributions are reported for individual questionnaire items.

Due to accepted convention the hypotheses are presented in the null form. However, as previous studies have reported their findings in very general terms, have not been sufficiently comparative, and have not engaged in hypothesis testing, there is an insufficient basis upon which to predict the expected direction that the findings would take.

> H1   Faculty members who are the heavier users of the library do not rely more significantly on the library's collection of government publications than do those who consult the library less frequently.

Data relating to this hypothesis, which were presented in the section of General Characteristics of Responding Faculty, indicate that the null hypothesis can be rejected. Faculty members who are heavy and moderate library users are more likely to be frequent documents users than those who are limited users and non-users of the library. However, as was already noted, data were skewed because responding faculty members are overwhelmingly frequent users of the library.

> H2   There is no statistically significant difference in the incidence of use of the library's documents collection between faculty members of institutions that grant the doctorate and those of institutions offering lesser degree programs.

As presented in the section on General Characteristics of Responding Faculty, highest degree offering is not a significant factor in use. Faculty members at baccalaureate and master's-granting institutions are as likely to use government publications as are their counterparts in doctorate-granting institutions. For example, all of the faculty respondents at one private baccalaureate institution utilize the library's collection of government publications at least to some degree.

H3   There is no statistically significant difference in the incidence of use of the library's documents collection between faculty members in one discipline and those in any of the other disciplines.

On the basis of the data, also presented in the section on General Characteristics of Responding Faculty, the null hypothesis was rejected. Chi square analysis indicated a statistically significant difference between disciplines and frequency of documents use. The finding that economists and political scientists are the heaviest users of government publications is consistent with research conducted earlier in Great Britain. The similarity in findings is presented in more detail in Chapter 6.

H4   Documents users within any one of the disciplines under study fall into similar areas of teaching specialties.

Each discipline was subdivided into standard, component parts reflecting different teaching options, and social scientists were asked to select from among the categories specified in an accompanying sheet the area of specialty reflected in their teaching. The investigator supplied the categories in an effort to control against a proliferation of specialties and against varying terminology. The categories used were also examined during the pretest and were modified so that they would be more representative of individual disciplines.

Social scientists often have more than one teaching specialty, and therefore any tallying of the combinations would yield a sum greater than 683, the total number of respondents. Given the small number of faculty members per department and the need to offer courses in the entire discipline, faculty members at baccalaureate institutions must teach a broad range of subjects. They are also more likely than their counterparts in graduate institutions to mark the "other" category for their teaching specialty. They teach survey courses in economics, history, political science, or sociology. Table 4-4 depicts the teaching specialties of responding social scientists. It might be noted that only the more frequently mentioned specialties from the "other" categories are presented in the table. For all of the disciplines except history, heavy use is spread out among all of the categories. As for history, those faculty members responsible for American history are the most likely to be heavy or moderate users; historians with other specialties, however, do make selective use of government publications.

H5   There is no statistically significant difference among faculty members as to their reasons for limited use or non-use of government publications.

As shown in Table 4-3, this null hypothesis was accepted. Regardless of discipline, highest degree offered, and institutional control, the major reason for infrequent use is that faculty members perceive themselves as being in fields in which government bodies publish little or nothing of value in their teaching

Table 4-4 Frequency of Documents Use (by Discipline)

	Types of Users[1]			
Discipline and Specialty	Heavy Number	Moderate Number	Limited Number	Non-User Number
1. Economics				
Comparative economic systems	3	4	2	—
Econometrics and statistics	12	7	6	2
Economic theory	23	18	8	5
History	7	6	4	1
Industrial organization	9	7	3	—
International economics	8	7	1	3
Labor and human resources development	11	10	4	—
Planning	1	3	1	—
Public finance	9	11	3	—
Urban economics	4	2	2	—
Other:				
Money and banking	6	3	—	2
Economics (in general)	2	3	3	—
Economic education	2	1	2	2
Economic development	1	2	2	1
2. History				
African	—	2	5	4
American	43	19	25	8
Ancient	—	—	1	5
Asian	1	2	5	5
British	—	1	5	9
Latin American	3	—	2	1
Medieval	1	—	3	9
Modern European	5	1	13	15
Russian, Soviet, and Eastern European	4	1	4	7
Other:				
World	2	—	1	1

[1] Heavy users are defined as those using the collection at least sixteen times last year. Moderate users consulted the collection between six and fifteen times, while limited users fell into the range of one to five times. Needless to say, non-users did not use the collection at all.

Table 4-4   (Continued)

Discipline and Specialty	Types of Users			
	Heavy Number	Moderate Number	Limited Number	Non-User Number
3. Political Science				
American politics	20	23	17	12
Comparative politics	12	10	10	6
International relations	12	13	10	—
Law	12	2	5	4
Public administration	7	7	3	1
Public policy	8	3	3	1
Political theory	4	5	7	6
Other:				
Research methods	1	2	1	1
Political science	—	1	2	—
4. Sociology				
Criminology	12	5	1	—
Deviance	5	4	3	2
Social organization	19	5	10	4
Social psychology	3	7	13	3
Theory	15	2	12	4
Urban sociology	5	5	2	1
Sociology of an area (i.e., family, religion, medicine, science, etc.)	23	11	16	6
Anthropology	3	2	10	3
Social work	4	2	3	—
Other:				
Research methods	25	2	7	1
Social change	1	1	6	3
Sociology	2	4	2	1
Population	4	2	—	—

and research interests. An important secondary reason for infrequent use is that the amount of time expended in locating relevant information in government publications is out of proportion to what can be found. It might be advantageous to interject a reminder that the purpose of the study was to describe and not to assess the accuracy of perceptions.

During the interview phase, those economists, political scientists, and sociologists dealing solely with theoretical subjects suggested that government publications do not provide the type of resources they need and that government publications deal more with public policy and other practical considerations. They suspect that their information requirements would be different if they scientifically tested theoretical conceptualizations. One economist in the area of intellectual history occasionally consults documents but more often relies on those reprinted in secondary sources.

As might be expected, historians dealing with time periods before the discovery of the United States have little need for publications produced by the governments under study. As has already been stated, social scientists dealing with American history seldom draw upon government publications, as such publications are seldom central to their professional needs. These historians are sometimes teaching survey courses or subjects such as intellectual or colonial history in which a different type of source material is needed. In one doctorate-granting institution a historian who specializes in New Deal politics occasionally consults the library's collection of government publications for statistical data or court cases. More often, however, he does not use the resources of the library at all, travelling instead to Washington, D.C., several times a year to use the National Archives and the Library of Congress. He also visits other eastern libraries and uses their documents collections; it does not matter to him that the same publications might be located at his university library. As he points out, he is familiar with these libraries and his need for government publications is sporadic.

Many social scientists have acquired personal copies of frequently used government publications. Price increases for publications of the Government Printing Office have forced some of them to reevaluate their purchases and to be more selective in their acquisitions; for others it has necessitated an increasing reliance on Congressional staffs in an effort to obtain needed publications gratis. Convenience is given as a major reason for having personal copies. Faculty members do not have to go to the library as frequently when they acquire their own documents. During the interviews, the author confirmed the acquisition of such personal copies by observing titles such as *County and City Data Book, Dictionary of Occupational Titles, Historical Statistics of the United States: Colonial Times to 1970,* and *Statistical Abstracts of the United States* in the book collections of survey subjects.

At this point, it is useful to cite two typical examples of faculty purchases of government publications. Each year one economist purchases the *Economic Report of the President.* He had subscribed to the *Monthly Labor Review* until his department began to receive it. From these two sources he gathers most of the statistical data for teaching. He finds that textbooks and monographic and periodical literature provide the necessary economic theory but that their statistical data are often outdated for class purposes. Therefore, he supplements those sources with the data contained in these two government publications.

A sociologist who described himself as an "inefficient user of libraries" obtains personal copies of all government publications which he suspects may be of immediate or potential benefit to his professional and recreational needs. He does this even if the library does have a copy. Occasionally he consults the library's documents collection, but only to browse among titles before ordering them. It is "more convenient [for him] to have source materials at home or in the office than to have to walk to the library," even though the library is located in close proximity to his office!

The investigator did not ask social scientists in either the questionnaire or interviews to rank the types of source material they draw upon for teaching, research, or community service. Many social scientists at baccalaureate and master's-granting institutions, where the primary mission related to teaching, seem to place government publications at a lower priority than they do monographic and periodical literature and commercial loose-leaf services. They feel that, in large part or entirely, periodical and monographic literature meet their needs. However, at another baccalaureate institution all of the social scientists make at least modest use of government publications contained in the library—if not for their own purposes, for those of their students. As all seniors at this institution are required to complete research projects in their subject majors, faculty members have to be alert to topics in which government publications might be applicable.

Some social scientists emphasized that it is easier for them to consult alternative sources of information; they suggested that government publications contain a vast amount of information, some of which might be potentially useful. However, it is too time-consuming to sift through government publications for the few relevant items. One economist at a graduate-level institution neither uses the library's documents collection nor monitors the release of new documents. He has professed satisfaction with the government publications that he had obtained four fears earlier while completing his dissertation. For current information he finds it easier to browse among such periodicals as the *Journal of Economic Literature*, extracting pertinent information.

Certain faculty members at baccalaureate institutions emphasized that their heavy teaching loads do not permit much opportunity for the pursuit of problems or issues in detail; with only a few assigned to teach in a given discipline, it is necessary for each to offer a variety of courses. They are not involved with graduate students and their courses are more general than intensive. Because of these circumstances they want easy access to desired information and need it in capsulized form. They find that government publications often provide more detail than is needed.

One political scientist, for example, relies on the *Congressional Quarterly Weekly Report* and other commercially produced loose-leaf services to provide information on current issues and events in summary form. He also draws heavily on newspapers and magazines for current capsulized information. As a community service, he does advisory work in the legal field. Here also his information is gained from the resources of a nongovernmental source, the West Publishing Company. The reference tools of this company are current and easily used, and they highlight the important court cases and issues, and the internal numbering system leads the user from one West publication to another.

In summary, it is useful to reiterate that the author is trying to describe and not to alter perceptions. Some of the infrequent users and non-users of government publications housed in the library appear satisfied with their limited access to information, even if that information may not be the most current and reliable. For example, one economist at a teaching institution makes little effort to search for current data, although his courses do center on current economic trends and policies. He prefers to update textbooks and monographic literature with capsulized data found in *Statistical Abstracts of the United States* and *U.S. News and World Report*. He claims that he does not go beyond the data contained in these sources.

> H6   Faculty members in one discipline do not differ significantly from those in any of the other disciplines as to the purposes for which they consult government publications.

In order to determine statistically if there is a relationship among disciplines, the author applied the Spearman Rank Order Correlation Coefficient test. It showed a moderate to strong relationship among the disciplines. There is a strong relationship between economics and political science (rho = .96), economics and sociology (rho = .99), history and sociology (rho = .90), and political science and sociology (rho = .90). Although the differences between history and sociology are not statistically significant, it was found that historians are much more likely to seek information of historical value while sociologists want research and technical reports. As depicted in Table 4-5, the top priority of economists and sociologists is to gather census or normative data; that of historians is to consult information of historical value; and that of political scientists is to keep abreast of current events and issues of interest or to seek census or normative data.

A moderate statistical relationship was found between history and political science (rho = .67), and economics and history (rho = .67). Historians emphasized information of historical value, whereas economists and political scientists, like sociologists, stressed research and technical reports. Political scientists checked the category of current events and issues of interest more than historians, economists, and sociologists.

Examination of the data by the variables of institutional control and highest degree offering revealed certain trends. As might be expected, faculty at doctorate-granting institutions are more likely to consult government publications for grant information (68.7 percent) than those at institutions with lesser degree programs. The use of documents for recreational reading matter is not evenly distributed among institutions and disciplines. At Michigan State Univer-

Table 4-5   Purposes for Which Documents Are Consulted

The Eight Purposes for Which Social Scientists Consulted Government Publications	Discipline				
	Economics	History	Political Science	Sociology	Total
Current events and issues of interest	76	43	78	67	264
Census or normative data	107	66	78	123	374
Information of historical value	56	113	63	57	289
Research and technical reports	91	32	76	113	312
Resources of value to students	65	49	66	72	252
Grant information	19	16	27	50	112
Recreational reading material	6	3	4	15	28
Other	2	–	3	–	5

sity six members of the department of Sociology checked this category, while economists and historians at public institutions indicated that they consult government publications for recreational reading matter although none of their counterparts at private institutions do. Additional differences arose in regard to institutional control and discipline. Of the sociologists using government-generated research and technical reports, 70.8 percent are located at public institutions; also, historians at public colleges and universities made greater use of documents for current events and issues of interest (69.8 percent), for research and technical reports (81.3 percent), and for resources of potential value to their students (73.5 percent), than do their counterparts at private institutions.

    H7   (a) Degree offered or discipline are not significant factors in accounting for how often faculty members seek assistance from library staff members; (b) frequency of documents use is not a significant factor in accounting for how often faculty members seek assistance from library staff members.

Of the social scientists utilizing government publications located in the library, more than half (351, or 61.5 percent) request assistance from the library staff only some of the time, whereas more than one-fourth (29.3 percent) *frequently* seek assistance. Approximately 6 percent of the users (thirty-three faculty members) never request assistance; a lesser percentage (twenty faculty members or 3.5 percent) always do.

Analysis of the data did not reveal any trends as far as institutional control and highest degree offered were concerned. Social scientists in lower degree programs are as likely to rely on library staff members as those in doctorate-granting institutions.

The chi square test indicated a statistically significant relationship between frequency of documents use and the frequency with which library staff are asked for assistance (χ^2 (3,4) = 701.81, $p >$ .01). A total of 61.2 percent of the heavy users sometimes request assistance, and 35.8 percent of this same group do so frequently. More than twice as many moderate documents users sometimes request assistance (64.7 percent) than do so frequently (29.4 percent). As for limited users, 59.1 percent of them sometimes request assistance, whereas 21 percent need help frequently. However, of those faculty members checking the category "always," 70 percent may be categorized as limited users.

Distinctions between categories of "never" and "sometimes," and "frequently" and "always" were not always clearly present. Operating on this assumption, the categories of "never" and "sometimes," and "frequently" and "always," were combined and these collapsed categories compared against the disciplines. Chi square analysis indicates a statistically significant difference (χ^2 (3,1) = 8.98, $p >$ .05), with 382, or 67.1 percent, of the users, regardless of discipline, requesting assistance a maximum of sometimes.

Of the four disciplines, sociologists are the least likely to request assistance. Approximately three-fourths of them (74.2 percent) request assistance no more than sometimes. Well over half of the political scientists (68.8 percent) and of the historians (65.2 percent) also request assistance infrequently. However, the percentage difference between those economists marking a maximum of "sometimes" (58.2 percent) and those checking either "frequently" or "always" was only 16.3. Therefore, economists are as likely to request assistance infrequently as they are to request it frequently. The important consideration then becomes "for what kinds of assistance do social scientists ask the library staff?"

> H8   There is no statistically significant difference between the frequency with which faculty members ask library staff for assistance and any reluctance on the part of faculty members to request it.

This null hypothesis was accepted due to the small percentage of faculty members who expressed reluctance in asking library staff members for assistance in using the collection and to the distribution of affirmative responses among all levels of documents users. Only forty-one, or 7.2 percent, of the social scientists who use documents express any reluctance to ask for assistance. Heavy users account for 24.4 percent (ten faculty) of those expressing reluctance while moderate users make up 31.7 percent (thirteen faculty), and limited users comprise 43.9 percent (eighteen faculty).

Further analysis of the forty-one respondents indicates that sixteen of them were associated with two institutions: a public master's-level institution and a private doctoral institution. With the inclusion of the other institutions, it was found that thirty-three of the respondents (80.5 percent) were faculty members of public master's-level and doctorate-granting institutions and private institutions offering the doctorate. Respondents were also examined on the basis of their discipline; however, no pattern emerged due to an even distribution among the four disciplines.

One questionnaire item asked faculty members to check those options which contribute to their reluctance. The major reasons were: the staff appears not well informed (24), consultation with staff does not lead to the desired government publications (21), the staff appears too busy to have time to deal with questions (21), the staff provides unsatisfactory service (13), and the reference questions of social scientists seem too elementary and the faculty members feel that they ought to know the answer (8). Two respondents pointed out that as they were usually in a hurry; they would not take the time to ask.

This hypothesis did not formally constitute an interview category due to the small percentage of social scientists who expressed reluctance in asking library staff members for assistance in using the collection. Those social scientists interviewed at all of the institutions except one emphasized the help-fulness of library staff members in finding needed publications. They appreciate the fact that librarians will search indexes and guides for them or alert them to new library acquisitions. Frequently the social scientists were unaware of the specific indexes searched but were impressed with the ability of librarians to find the needed citations.

At the one institution which was the exception, two of the twelve inter-view subjects, both limited users of government publications, emphasized that certain library staff members provide discourteous and incomplete service to their students. They would refer students to specific titles in the documents department, but the students would return and complain that whoever was on duty in the department was unaware of the location of sources such as *United States Statutes at Large* and the *United States Code*. Now the two social scientists accompany their students and point out the location of the sources. Although the author did not attempt to verify the accuracy of these perceptions, it should be noted that the institution with which these two social scientists were affiliated was one at which questionnaire respondents also indicated the existence of a service problem. In fact, the library's annual report called atten-tion to the problem but suggested that it had been remedied; apparently such was not the case!

H9   (a) Social scientists do not differ significantly according to discipline or highest degree offered as to the kinds of assistance that they ask from the library staff; (b) they are no more likely to approach library staff for assist-ance in locating a specific document than they are to request reference assistance (that is, aid in finding materials or information to answer a specific question or solve some problem on which they are working).

A methodological note might be inserted: the categories for kinds of assistance do not comprise discrete, separate entities, except for those dealing with reference assistance and the ordering of documents not contained in the collection. There may be a fine distinction between help in locating a specific document and assistance in finding documents not located on the shelf; nevertheless, the Spearman Rank Order Correlation Coefficient method indicates a perfect, positive monotonic relationship among historians, political scientists, and sociologists. The relationship between economists and historians, political scientists, and sociologists is also strong (a rho of .94 in each case). The null hypothesis [H9(a)] was accepted.

There was an even distribution of responses as to disciplines, institution, and highest degree offering. As depicted in Table 4-6, social scientists request assistance for a variety of reasons. The most important reason is that they need help in locating a specific document. Reference assistance was the second ranked kind of help requested by historians, political scientists, and sociologists; however, it was ranked third by economists. It should be noted that 103 faculty members, evenly distributed by discipline and frequency of documents use, approach the library staff to order for the library a government publication not contained in the collection. Fifty-six of these faculty are heavy documents users, whereas twenty-one of the remaining forty-seven social scientists are limited users.

On the basis of these findings, H9(b) can be accepted. Social scientists are as likely to approach library staff for assistance in locating a specific document as they are to request reference assistance.

The significance of the findings in relation to both hypotheses is twofold. First of all, there is a similarity of responses across disciplines and institutions. Economists, for example, comprise the heaviest users of government publications and are the group most likely to seek assistance. However, their requests for assistance do not take any one form but reflect diverse needs and interests

Table 4-6   Kinds of Assistance Requested by Faculty

Kinds	Number of Responses
Help in locating a specific government publication	489
Reference assistance	305
Assistance in finding government publications not located on the shelf	259
Assistance in locating government publications not held by the library	168
Help in ordering for the library a government publication not contained in the collection	103

ranging from locating a source not currently on the shelf to aiding the library staff in collection-building. Second, frequency of documents use is not a significant variable. Heavy, moderate, and limited users responded in a similar manner on each choice.

H10 (a) Social scientists do not differ significantly across disciplines or institutions as to their means of locating needed government publications; (b) for access to government information held in the library, they rely primarily on the public card catalog or citations to documents found in the general literature or special bibliographies of their subject field.

As depicted in Table 4-7, social scientists locate needed government publications through a variety of means, the most important of which is by finding citations in the general and bibliographic literature of their subject field. Chi square analysis shows that there is no statistically significant difference between the methods used and highest degree offered in their institutions, frequency of library use, and institutional control.

The Spearman Rank Order method indicates strong to perfect relationships between pairs of ranked data—those representing the disciplines. Therefore, the null hypothesis for H10(a) is accepted. A perfect, positive relationship was evident between economists and historians, and a strong, positive relationship with political scientists (rho = .97) and sociologists (rho = .95). There was also a strong relationship between historians and political scientists (rho = .97), historians and sociologists (rho = .95), and political scientists and sociologists (rho = .90).

Although no discipline differed significantly as to search patterns, it might be beneficial to observe similarities. Regardless of discipline, the most important means for locating desired documents is by finding citations in the general

Table 4-7 Means by Which Social Scientists Locate Needed Documents

Means	Number
Finding citations to documents in the general literature or special bibliographies in their subject field	289
Consulting indexes of govenment publications	254
Relying on sources already familiar to them	250
Consulting the public card catalog	240
Browsing in areas of the collection relevant to their interests	177
Finding references in newspapers	59
Receiving citations to documents from the library staff	57
Other	5

literature or special bibliographies of the subject field. Historians and economists rely next most frequently on the indexes to government publications, whereas political scientists listed this option third, and sociologists checked it fourth. Political scientists ranked a reliance on a source already familiar to them as the second-most important category, whereas the other social scientists felt this category ranked third. The public card catalog rated fourth for economists, historians, and political scientists, but second for sociologists.

The Superintendent of Documents Classification Scheme, which is based on the principle of provenance, may not group all works of a similar subject and by the same personal author together under the same general notation. In addition, governmental departments and agencies publish on diverse topics, not all of which are commonly associated with particular departments or agencies. For these reasons, a commonly held assumption is that separately housed collections of documents are difficult to browse in.

For this study, browsing in areas of the collection relevant to particular faculty interests was listed as one of the options for locating needed documents. Regardless of discipline, social scientists listed it as the fifth choice.

The final two questionnaire categories presented to the social scientists received a range from nine to twenty-one checks per discipline. These infrequently mentioned choices are the location of references in newspapers and the receipt of citations to documents from the library staff.

Social scientists interviewed, realizing the limitations of the card catalog, rely most frequently on the subject literature. For some of them, consulting the card catalog is a wasted step in the literature search process; few government publications are cataloged, and these are mainly reference publications, periodicals, and popular and general titles. These may not be the types of government publications needed by the social scientists. Instead of the card catalog, they rely on the documents staff members, indexes, or browsing.

One interview subject would have liked libraries to list their government publications in the main card catalog—primarily in the section for titles. Inclusion in the author section was not deemed necessary because of the cumbersome format of main entries. The other social scientists suspected that the expenses involved in cataloging would prevent libraries from listing even government publications by title.

Since browsing patterns for government publications have not been reported in library literature, it may be interesting to describe those of the four social scientists who listed this as a means for locating publications: one of them consults indexes to government publications, identifies several relevant citations, and then browses in the shelves in the proximity of where that Superintendent of Documents' Classification (SUDOC) number falls. For him, this method is easier than laboring through many issues of an index and checking with library staff members just to determine if the library holds the desired publications.

For one economist, browsing constitutes the major means for locating government publications; he does not use indexes because they supply numerous sources not held by his baccalaureate institution. He checks citations in his subject literature instead, noting the issuing governmental body such as the Department of Health, Education and Welfare. Whenever he is unfamiliar with the SUDOC number for that department or agency, he asks the library staff members for it. With this information he proceeds to the shelf and examines all the publications for that governmental body; if he is unsure of issuing agencies, he guesses and browses in that particular area. In response to the interview question as to what library staff members might do to assist him, he suggested that they might supply him "with a list of SUDOC stem numbers to facilitate more systematic browsing."

The final two browsers rely only on the publications of selected Federal agencies. They do not consult source material beyond this, and they are familiar with the types of publishing done by these agencies. Therefore, they feel that indexes would not really be helpful to them.

In summary, there is no statistical difference among disciplines as to the means by which faculty members locate needed information. Although not statistically significant, social scientists across disciplines rank the use of the general literature and special subject bibliographies within their fields as the primary means by which they learn about sources. Consulting the public card catalog is considerably less important for all of the disciplines except sociology. More important reasons for economists, historians, and political scientists, although not statistically significant, are that they rely on sources already familiar to them and that they consult the indexes to government documents. Therefore, it becomes important which indexes are consulted. This topic will be analyzed later in this chapter.

Before concluding a discussion of the findings relating to these two hypotheses, an observation should be noted. An analysis of the different means used for locating needed documents does not suggest the value or usefulness of the information discovered by each approach. However, the analysis does indicate the relative importance that social scientists attach to each method.

> H11   There is no statistically significant difference among faculty members as to how they learned to find materials in the documents collection.

In answer to a query regarding how they learn to find materials in the documents collection, not all faculty members limited their responses to one category. Only twenty-nine of them had taken formal courses involving documents utilization. The rest of the respondents rely on less formal approaches centering on trial-and-error processes in actually using the collection (389), informal instruction from the library staff members (209), and self-instruction—by reading manuals or guides to the use of documents (141).

The null hypothesis was accepted. There was no statistically significant difference as to highest degree offered by the institution, frequency of library use, institutional control, and discipline, but an examination of the data on institutional bases did indicate some variations. Seventeen respondents at private baccalaureate institutions had used the trial-and-error approach, but for some reason only one of them was a member of the faculty at Principia College. Viewed from a different perspective, only six social scientists at private baccalaureate institutions had engaged in self-instruction as a means for finding materials in the documents collection. The rest were more likely to adopt the trial-and-error approach or to receive informal instruction from the library staff.

> H12   There is no statistically significant difference across discipline, highest degree offered, or institutional control as to the levels of government of which publications are used.

The Spearman Rank Order method, which was used to test for a difference among disciplines, indicated that there is a strong relationship among the levels of government of which publications were consulted and economics and history (rho = .98), economics and political science (rho = .98), history and sociology (rho = .98), and political science and sociology (rho = .98). There was a perfect, positive relationship between economics and sociology, and history and political science.

Regardless of discipline, publications of the United States government receive the most interest (562 faculty), those of the United Nations and other international agencies the next (270 faculty), and those of state governments the median (229 faculty). The publications of foreign governments (197 faculty) and municipal governments (79 faculty) receive less support. Although not statistically significant, there is some variation across disciplines as to the use of state and foreign government publications. Economists and sociologists rate publications of state governments third most important, whereas historians and political scientists believe that foreign government publications rank third.

Although the publications of one level of government received a certain number of checks, this did not indicate the relative frequency with which respondents use them. Social scientists were asked not only to check as many options as applied but also to order them in terms of frequency of use with number 1 for the greatest use, number 2 for the next greatest, etc. However, as approximately half of the respondents merely checked appropriate levels without assigning values to them, any analysis of frequency of use would be incomplete and misleading.

No statistically significant relationships emerged from a comparison between the various levels of government consulted and discipline, frequency of documents use, highest degree offered by the institution, and type of institutional control. However, the data contained in Table 4-8 indicate some variation within the baccalaureate institutions for the publications of international organi-

Table 4-8　Comparison of Levels of Government Consulted to Institutional Control and Highest Degree Offering

| | Levels of Government | | | | |
Institutions	Federal (Number)	State (Number)	Municipal (Number)	Foreign (Number)	International Agencies (Number)
Public B.A.	17	11	3	3	7
Public M.A.	130	68	22	33	47
Public Ph.D.	218	79	25	85	105
Private B.A.	24	9	3	9	15
Private M.A.	51	21	9	12	24
Private Ph.D.	122	41	17	55	72
Total	562	229	79	197	270

zations and foreign governments; faculty members at private baccalaureate institutions use such documents more than do their counterparts at public institutions. While some social scientists at baccalaureate institutions consulted municipal government publications, there are two schools, Indiana University, Kokomo, and Hanover College, where there was no use reported. One other point is worth noting. According to the groupings in Table 4-8, the number of faculty members consulting publications of municipal governments ranged from three to twenty-five. Publications of municipal governments do not comprise major informational resources for those social scientists studied.

H13　There is no statistically significant difference between faculty members engaged in sponsored research projects and those who are not as to their use of computerized search systems that access government information contained in bibliographic or numeric data bases.

H14　There is no statistically significant difference between the source of funding and whether or not machine-readable data bases are searched.

H15　Social scientists do not differ significantly across highest degree offered or discipline as to the specific search system(s) used.

A study of government publications must take into consideration the fact that not all of the information is published in the form of books, pamphlets, or audio-visuals. An increasing amount of data, statistical and bibliographical, collected and disseminated by government agencies is becoming available to the public in machine-readable form. As a result, faculty members were queried as to whether they use search systems (computerized or manual) that access government information contained in data bases. Only 8.4 percent of the documents users replied to this question in the affirmative.

These faculty members are clustered in doctorate-granting institutions, public and private, and public master's-level institutions; approximately three-fourths of them (70.8 percent) are members of either political science or sociology departments. Historians account for only 8.3 percent of the users. This finding is not surprising given the emphasis of these search systems on current, rather than retrospective, information. Only one faculty member from a baccalaureate institution, an economist, used a search system. This social scientist constituted one of the interview subjects, and his comments are reported below. Over half of the faculty members consulting a search system (61.2 percent) comprise heavy documents users while the remaining percentage is almost evenly divided between moderate (20.4 percent) and limited (18.4 percent) users.

As shown in Table 4-9, the most frequently mentioned search system is one exploiting the ERIC files for information in *Resources in Education* and *Current Index to Journals in Education*. This system is used especially by sociologists and economists, while only two historians and two political scientists reported consulting it. Use of the Census Tapes, the next most frequently checked system, is distributed among all the disciplines, with the largest number of users in sociology. The other search systems are used to lesser degrees. Even AcCIS, which provides access to information contained in Congressional and statistical publications, is infrequently consulted.

The literature of library and information science, as well as discussions at conventions, reflect a concern as to whether or not libraries should charge users (and if so, how much) for using search systems. However, there is little published data on the number of users consulting search systems involving fees-for-service. For this study, faculty members utilizing search systems were asked to specify whether or not their searches involve fees; for 33.3 percent of them, it does. The rest of the respondents utilize systems involving no charge.

As was noted in the section on General Characteristics of Responding Faculty (Chapter 2), many faculty members receive financial support for sponsored research. Some 85.4 percent of the users of search systems receive

Table 4-9   Computerized Search Systems Used by Social Scientists

Specific System Used	Number
ERIC search	21
Census Tapes (U.S. Bureau of the Census)	15
NTISearch (National Technical Information Service)	8
MEDLINE	7
SSIE (Smithsonian Science Information Exchange)	6
AcCIS (On-line information retrieval to Congressional Information Service publications)	5
CAIN/AGRICOLA (Agricultural On-Line Access)	2
Other	7

financial support for sponsored research, and the distribution between those engaged and those not engaged in nonsponsored research is approximately the same. Given the small number of faculty members using search systems and the small percentage of social scientists participating in fee-for-service searches, apparently few faculty members avail themselves of documents search systems as expenditure items for sponsored research. It might be, of course, that they consult nongovernmental machine-readable files.

To summarize questionnaire findings, only a small percentage of the respondents employ search systems. These respondents, primarily political scientists and sociologists, are not confined to faculty members engaged in sponsored research. There was insufficient data to analyze fully H14. The author could not detect a difference between the source of funding and the searching of machine-readable data bases. It would seem that due to the small number of data base users, funding generated by the Federal government does not result in more extensive use of data bases. In fact, only two search systems, one to the ERIC files and the other to the Census Tapes, receive general use.

Five of the social scientists interviewed (7.4 percent) use data bases; all but one of them are located at doctoral institutions. The exception, an economist, is located at a baccalaureate institution; he, however, had found a search of the ERIC system unsatisfactory as most of the bibliographic citations were to sources not held by his library or by libraries in close proximity. He did *not* avail himself of interlibrary loan as the process was too slow and the loan period too short.

The other four social scientists, all of whom use Census Tapes, represent all the disciplines except history.[5] Two of the users of Census Tapes had consulted Public Use Tapes for their local Standard Metropolitian Statistical Area (SMSA), while a third user had manipulated Public Use Tapes for a national sample. The final social scientist, a sociologist, had obtained Public Use Tapes specifying ethnic and racial designations. He bought his own tapes because the available statistical data on Mexican-Americans is sparse. However, as the 1980 Census plans greater coverage of ethnic groups, he will not be able to afford to purchase tapes out of his own income. The cost, if he is to obtain the tapes at all, will have to be carried by sponsored research grants.

With the exception of tapes used by this one sociologist, tapes had been purchased with departmental funds or from grants relating to sponsored research. These tapes are stored in faculty offices, departmental laboratories, or, in one case, in a campus institute. They are frequently used by other members of the department for their research activities.

The central problem, according to interview subjects, is one of bibliographic control. Faculty members are unaware of tapes held by other departments on

[5]The Bureau of the Census has prepared for sale Public Use Tape files containing samples of individual records from the 1960 and 1970 Census of Population and Housing by removing all information that might identify persons or households.

campus or of the range of tapes which can be purchased. Because of this, they believe that their university libraries have a responsibility to acquire, house, and instruct faculty members and students in the use of data bases. They recommend that library staff members prepare codebooks and have the programming expertise necessary to assist users in data manipulation. If such a role is too expensive for libraries, they should, as a minimum, identify those data bases held on the campus, at other institutions, and in the government, and disseminate this information to the faculty members.

While this section has focused on the reasons for use of data bases, bibliographic and numeric, brief mention might be made of some of the reasons for *not* using this resource. Reasons include lack of need for such specialized data for teaching, cost factors, lack of ready access to the government publications cited, and the ability to find comparable information in alternative sources.

H16   There is no statistically significant difference among faculty members as to which specific indexes are consulted.

H17   Among all of the indexes, faculty members consult the *Monthly Catalog of U.S. Government Publications* most frequently

These hypotheses are concerned with the range of indexes that social scientists consult. No attempt was made to gauge the frequency of use per title, the type of information sought, or the value of each index for specific search strategies.

Research conducted by Hernon and Williams (1976) had found that social scientists "have limited familiarity with the indexes and abstracts and rely primarily on the *Monthly Catalog of U.S. Government Publications,* ERIC *Resources in Education,* and the [now] defunct *Price Lists*" (1976, 98). The faculty members surveyed by them had little awareness of other indexes. In addition, it was found that "of the social scientists who use documents, thirty (29 percent) of them were unfamiliar with any of the appropriate indexes" (Hernon & Williams, 1976, 98).

The present study found that 160, or 28 percent, of the documents users do not consult any indexes. Seventy-four of them are limited users, while the remaining percentages are evenly distributed among heavy (47) and moderate (39) users.

As depicted in Table 4-10, a comparatively small number of titles are checked frequently. The *Monthly Catalog* was not the most frequently mentioned title. It ranked second after the *Index to U.S. Government Periodicals;* ERIC *Resources in Education* rated ninth on the list, while *Selected U.S. Government Publications,* a free guide listing current and popular sales publications of the Government Printing Office, came in third. Twenty-one social scientists marked the "other" category and included, among other titles, the *Bureau of the Census Catalog* and listings of the National Archives, Agricultural Department, Labor Department, and LEAA National Criminal Justice Informa-

Table 4-10   Guides and Indexes Consulted by Faculty

Titles	Number
Index to U.S. Government Periodicals	195
Monthly Catalog of U.S. Government Publications	180
Selected U.S. Government Publications	125
Historical indexes including "Documents Catalog" *(Catalog of the Public Documents of the 53rd to 76th Congress and All Departments of the Government . . .);* "Tables and Index" *(Tables of, and Annotated Index to the Congressional Series of U.S. Public Documents, 15th to 52nd Congress);* Ames' *Comprehensive Index to the Publications of the U.S. Government, 1881-1893;* Poore's *Descriptive Catalog of the Government Publications of the U.S., Sept. 5, 1774-March 4, 1881;* and *Checklist of U.S. Public Documents*	124
CIS (Congressional Information Service) *Index*	80
PAIS (Public Affairs Information Service) *Bulletin*	77
Government Reports Announcement & Index	70
American Statistics Index	67
ERIC Resources in Education	57
Declassified Documents Catalog	26
Index Medicus	18
CIS US Serial Set Index	17
Selected Water Resources Abstracts	9
Technical Abstracts Bulletin	7
Transdex (index to JPRS publications)	6
U.S. Geological Survey Publications indexes	6
Air Pollution Abstracts	4
Nuclear Science Abstracts/Atomindex	3
Scientific Technical Aerospace Reports	1
Other	21

tion and Statistics Service. One social scientist wrote that he receives weekly and monthly newsletters in the health area which contain references to government publications.

Chi square analysis indicates a statistically significant difference between frequency of library use and index titles (χ^2 (2,19) = 39.24, $p > .01$) and between institutions having graduate and baccalaureate programs, and index titles (χ^2 (1,19) = 41.09, $p > .01$). As would be expected, social scientists at doctorate-granting institutions list more indexes. This finding is understandable given the cost to libraries of subscribing to the indexes, many of which are commercially produced and therefore expensive.

Analysis of the specific titles consulted by faculty members at each institution reinforces the finding that social scientists at graduate institutions consult more index titles than do those at baccalaureate institutions. Certain indexes such as those produced by the Congressional Information Service and the ERIC clearinghouse were listed by few, if any, faculty members associated with baccalaureate institutions. These indexes were more frequently mentioned by social scientists at graduate institutions.

The Spearman Rank Order test, which was used as a means for determining similarities of index use among disciplines, indicated moderate agreement between economics and history (rho = .75), economics and political science (rho = .86), economics and sociology (rho = .77), history and political science (rho = .88), history and sociology (rho = .74), and political science and sociology (rho = .73).

Forty, or 58.8 percent, of the social scientists interviewed do not consult indexes, emphasizing instead that they do not need indexes to meet their information requirements. For them government publications can be obtained outside the library, or by relying on library sources already familiar to them, browsing, or consulting library staff members. For example, one political scientist who makes extensive use of Congressional hearings does not use indexes. Instead he guesses which committee has responsibility for a particular problem and writes to a member of that committee, he browses in the library shelves, or he holds the question until he makes his annual visit to the Library of Congress!

Ten interview subjects had used the *Monthly Catalog* since the change in format, which began with the July 1976 issue.[6] These social scientists welcome the increased size of the monthly issues as they assume that this reflects more comprehensive coverage. They find the *Monthly Catalog* easier to use but note that they must schedule a large block of time when using the index because searching generally cannot be done quickly. It might be hypothesized that they have been conditioned by past experiences and have learned to accept the problems with the use of indexes.

The major weakness of indexes, as suggested by the social scientists, is the time lag between public availability of a publication and its coverage by indexes. Because of this problem, social scientists find that they must build flexibility into their search strategies. Apparently, indexes do not constitute a primary resource for current information—that issued within the past year. To lessen the impact of the time lag, social scientists are receptive to current awareness services which highlight publications shortly before or after publication. Of course such services may only resolve half of the problem. Libraries still need to acquire and process new sources faster.

[6]The Superintendent of Documents joined the Ohio College Library Center's (OCLC) on-line cataloging network, converted to the MARC format, and changed the *Monthly Catalog* to the Anglo-American cataloging rules.

H18 There is no statistically significant difference among faculty members according to highest degree offered, discipline, institutional control, or frequency of documents use as to the means by which they locate the publications of (a) the United States government; (b) state governments; and (c) municipal governments.

Federal Government

Previous use studies of Federal government publications have found that faculty members rely predominantly on the general and bibliographic literature of their subject field and that they receive citations from their colleagues. However, these studies did not compare disciplines and use among publications of different levels of government. As with the preceding hypothesis, no attempt was made to determine either the frequency by which faculty members use a particular approach to documents or the quality of the information received.

As shown in Table 4-11, faculty members in general locate Federal documents from citations in the general literature or in special bibliographies of their subject fields. Responses indicated that social scientists are not dependent on library resources for their information. They rely on the general and bibliographic literature of their subject field, mailing lists, colleagues, and they contact agencies as means of fulfilling many of their information needs. In the "other" category, social scientists explained that they contact their representatives in Congress or the clerk of the Supreme Court for information, visit the nearest Government Printing Office (GPO) bookstore, or check references in testimony submitted in Congressional hearings.

Table 4-11   Means by Which Federal Publicatons Are Located

Means	Number
Finding citations in the general literature or special bibliographies in their subject field	368
Being on mailing lists of Federal agencies	262
Receiving citations from colleagues	215
Contacting Federal agencies	182
Receiving assistance from libraries	163
Browsing through selection aids such as *Selected U.S. Government Publications*	142
Drawing on resources of professional societies	125
Checking newspapers	120
Drawing on resources of associations	82
Other	10

One economist wrote that each year he gains awareness of government publications in the area of public finance by contacting Federal agencies and professional societies, drawing on the advice of professional societies, finding citations in the general and bibliographic literature of the subject field, receiving citations from colleagues, and receiving assistance from librarians. He sifts through all of the titles brought to his attention and purchases from the Government Printing Office five to ten of the publications which are not too expensive and which he plans to consult frequently; he thereby minimizes his dependence on the documents collection housed in the library.

One sociologist detailed the role that newspapers play in his literature searches. He scans the *New York Times* and *Christian Science Monitor* for information pertaining to his research and teaching interests. He noted that he would "make greater use of documents if these newspapers gave complete references when they reported on publications." He has even written to the staff of the *New York Times* about the problem and received the reply that "they could not include complete references with each article." A historian, a member of the American Committee on the History of the Second World War, indicated that the Committee's semiannual *Newsletter* has a bibliography section which, in part, alerts readers to important government publications.

Responses to each of the categories given in Table 4-11 were not evenly distributed among institutions. However, there is no statistically significant difference between institutions offering the doctorate and those offering other degree programs (χ^2 (1,9) = 9.71, $p < .05$).

The Spearman Rank Order method indicates a moderate agreement between economics and history (rho = .70), but strong agreement among the other disciplines (rho ranging from .96 to .98). Regardless of discipline, social scientists checked the category of finding citations in the general and bibliographic literature of their subject field most frequently. Although variations in rankings were not statistically significant, they do reflect some differences in emphasis. Economists, political scientists, and sociologists rely the next most frequently on materials received from mailing lists of Federal agencies, while historians mark this category fourth. For historians the second most important source of citations is their colleagues. Economists and political scientists place this category fourth, whereas sociologists label it third. Reliance on assistance from librarians receives more support from historians than from the other social scientists—historians list it third while the others place it between fifth and eighth.

Some recent studies have attempted to determine the comparative importance of different methods of locating information. These studies have found that browsing among books and journals comprises the major means by which scientists learn about other sources. Recommendations of colleagues ranks as the second most frequently used method, while citations in the literature and in indexes are considerably less important. (Voigt, 1961, pp. 5-6).

Although there is variation among the categories used, it is evident from the discussion relating to this hypothesis that social scientists have different search patterns from scientists. For social scientists citations in the general literature are much more important than browsing.

The interview phase confirmed questionnaire findings. However, variation was noted and it resulted from two factors: (1) the recency of the information sought, and (2) the likelihood that libraries would have the types of publications needed. The faculty members interviewed do not have uniform need for all types of Federal publications. In fact, they seem to concentrate heavily on a few types. These are statistical data, primarily those of the Bureau of the Census, census reports, Congressional hearings,[7] Congressional committee prints, reports of investigations conducted by Federal agencies and special commissions, annual reports, court cases, and foreign policy materials. More specifically, the clustering of responses among a relatively few titles suggests that perhaps a core literature of government publications might be constructed for certain disciplines across the social sciences. This literature might comprise the following titles which interview subjects repeatedly suggest they subscribe to or gather information from on a regular basis. (It should be pointed out that the investigator did not circulate a list of titles among interview subjects. Titles reported emerged during the interviews.)

> *Business Digest*
> *Congressional Record* and its predecessors
> *Consumer Price Index*
> *County and City Data Book*
> *Current Population Reports*
> *Economic Report of the President*
> *Employment and Earnings*
> *Federal Reserve Bulletin*
> *Foreign Broadcast Information Service* (FBIS) *Daily Reports*
> *Foreign Relations of the United States*
> *Historical Statistics of the United States: Colonial Times to 1970*
> *Monthly Labor Review*
> *State Department Bulletin*
> *Statistical Abstracts of the United States*
> *Survey of Current Business*
> *Treasury Bulletin*

Other selected serial titles from the Departments of Labor and Treasury might be added to this list.

The emphasis of most of these publications is on current information.

---

[7]It was pointed out that the Appendices to hearings contain information which cannot be found elsewhere. At times, social scientists have discovered information in the Appendices which Federal agencies had previously refused to supply them. The agencies later made this information available to members of Congress.

They provide a means for economists, political scientists, and sociologists to update textbooks and monographic and periodical literature for their teaching. For example, if a student finds the theory behind international trade in textbooks, but only dated supportive statistical data there, he can turn to sources such as the *Survey of Current Business* for *current* statistical data. However for other teaching and research needs, such sources seem unlikely to provide recent enough information or the type needed.

Many of the social scientists interviewed make only selective use of the government publications collection. Often it is for statistical data or for items too expensive for them to own personally. Three sociologists found the library's arrangement of government publications confusing and not easily understood; it was easier to avoid problems, consult the *Selected U.S. Government Publications,* and order personal copies as long as the expense involved was minimal. As is evident, social scientists often do not consult a wide range of government publishing. Their library use appears to focus on selected types, primarily on those of a statistical nature, and on the publications of selected executive departments and agencies, and on legislative committees. They supplement, or bypass, their institutional library's documents collection by querying Federal officials about specific policies, programs, and activities, or by obtaining personal copies of documents, some of which they suspect are not being gathered at all in libraries or at least within the time frame they need.

Forty, or 58.8 percent, of the social scientists seek current information and suggested that libraries either are not collecting all of the types of publications they rely upon or that the publications are too old to meet their needs by the time libraries place them on the shelves. They require government publications soon after their public release. As to the types of current publications consulted, they draw upon texts of speeches, press conferences, and news releases distributed by selected departments or agencies. Such ephemeral sources might be more valuable to them than a list of publications, as these sources suggest current policy positions, changes, and issues. These public announcements are often distributed by the State Department (Bureau of Public Affairs. Office of Public Communication), Bureau of Labor Statistics, and Department of Energy.[8]

Mailing lists constitute an important means by which those social scientists interviewed become aware of new publications. In addition to public announcements, they sometimes also receive lists of publications or complimentary copies sent from specific agencies or Congressional committees. The National Criminal Justice Reference Service, for example, operates an international clearinghouse for criminal justice information and distributes "Selective Notification of Infor-

---

[8]One of these sources was *Information: Weekly Announcements* (Department of Energy. Office of Public Affairs). It contains brief reports for the news media of what is occurring within the Department. The items reported do not duplicate *DOE Headquarters Public Announcements,* which carries news releases.

mation," which announces sources of information, seminars, and meetings pertaining to law enforcement and criminal justice. Social scientists can order sources directly through this service. These notices may provide prepublication announcements, in which case social scientists can get the items soon after their public release. Publications may also be emphasized by the associations of specific disciplines. The Population Association of America (PAA) has a monthly newsletter, for example, which contains a section on new Federal publications of interest to demographers.

Social scientists within and across disciplines do not have a uniform need for government publications. Some of the factors affecting their frequency of documents use appear to be: the institutional mission, the subject area covered, whether or not their courses are introductory, the number of courses taught per academic year,[9] perceived value of government information in relation to other source material, previous experience in using a documents department, and the extent of faculty involvement in research. For some the need for government publications may be more of a sporadic than a continual nature. They may make extensive use of government publications for a relatively short time and then not need to consult them again for a long time. One social scientist draws heavily upon statistical data on a regular basis but only infrequently uses any other type of document, such as Congressional hearings. For him an occasional list of hearings received by the library would be invaluable; the monographic and periodical literature of political science provides the main access point to hearings; he does not consult indexes at all. One economist, also with an occasional need for government publications, discovers sources from the footnotes of his students' papers. He follows up references if titles sound promising or if he wants to challenge a student's interpretation. Four of the social scientists suggested that their literature search processes depend on their familiarity with a subject area and its source material. If they are familiar with the area, they rely on sources already familiar to them; however, if they venture into a new area, they rely on the documents librarian for assistance.

Initially the investigator concluded each interview by asking participants if there is anything that a library or government could do to help them become aware of new information sources or gain ready access to them. It soon became apparent, however, that few participants had concrete suggestions, perhaps because they had never thought about the subject before. Respondents are either satisfied with their present level of access to government publications or they want assistance. Those requesting assistance favor a list of new document

[9]One teacher of modern European history had noted references to publications of the United States government, especially those dealing with foreign relations, in the subject literature of his field. However, he had not searched for them because foreign policy issues were not central to his research interests. He explained that as the only teacher of modern European history at the institution he is unable to pursue topics not relevant to his immediate interests.

acquisitions for the library. Few of them want a list of documents not held by the library because it is too time-consuming to acquire them. Some emphasized that they already receive more than they have time to peruse, while others stressed the need to examine more information that might pertain to their research interests. Five faculty members pointed out that as their subject specialization is interdisciplinary in nature, they cannot depend on current awareness services having narrow focuses. These findings suggest that libraries cannot rely on one such service but must take into consideration diverse needs.

Several of the interview subjects asked if libraries compile lists of Federal agencies and Congressional committees which distribute public announcements, since they want to get on the mailing lists. They doubt that libraries should collect such ephemera, but they favor the idea of libraries disseminating them as current awareness items to be discarded once interested faculty members have perused them.

In summary, social scientists resort to a variety of methods to obtain needed government information. They do not expect depository libraries to have all of the materials needed. In fact, they suggest that time lags between the issuance of a publication and its availability in libraries necessitate adopting search techniques of their own to acquire the publication. They draw upon mailing lists and contact with governmental officials and members of Congressional staffs, some of whom are their former students.[10] With the indexing time lag, sources such as the *Monthly Catalog* sometimes fail as primary access points to needed publications.[11] Indexes also do not pick up the types of current information sources they draw upon, such as press releases and public announcements. Newspapers sometimes contain some of these, but they sometimes lack verbatim texts; therefore, the mailing lists of the State Department and Department of Energy fill vital roles in meeting the information requirements of social scientists. Libraries often play supportive roles. They enable social scientists to use government publications which they can get elsewhere only with difficulty. In some cases, social scientists are willing to wait until the library receives the needed government publication (depending on how central the information source is to their immediate needs), although in other cases they search for alternative sources containing similar information. These need not be government publications.

[10] One historian queries the Historical Office of the State Department, the National Security Council, and the Defense Department for access to information on the origins of the Korean War. If the material has been classified, he invokes the Freedom of Information Act. Although it may take a while, he is usually successful in getting the requested material as long as he is able to describe specific dispatches and their dates. Primary sources such as the papers of General Douglas MacArthur may describe messages between the command office in Japan and the government in Washington. Sufficient information is provided on which he can base his requests.

[11] The *Publications Reference File*, which is a microfiche listing of new and current Government Printing Office publications, might cut down on the time lag. However, social scientists interviewed were unfamiliar with this new source.

State Government

As mentioned in H12, faculty members were queried as to what levels of government produce the publications that they use. Some 229 or 40.1 percent, of the documents users reported consulting state publications, which means that the publications of this level of government are checked the third most frequently.

Table 4-12 depicts the methods by which social scientists in each discipline locate needed state government publications. As a group, social scientists indicated that their major methods are those of finding citations in the general literature or special bibliographies of their subject field, contacting state agencies, and receiving citations from colleagues. Receiving assistance from librarians ranks fourth while consulting such general indexes as the Library of Congress' *Monthly Checklist of State Publications* or specific state checklists rates lower priority. Checking newspapers was mentioned more frequently than consulting indexes. Perhaps the explanation for this is that social scientists come across pertinent information by chance, from a perusal of the mass media. In the "other" category, social scientists suggested that their departments and colleagues have resources which they can tap and that they rely on friends or research assistants in state government.

The Spearman Rank Order method was also used to analyze the data depicted in Table 4-12. It indicates strong agreement between economists and political scientists (rho = .92), political scientists and sociologists (rho = .92), and economists and sociologists (rho = .83). Both economists and political scientists list as their primary methods for locating state publications, first of all, citations in the general and bibliographic literature and, second, contacting state agencies. Sociologists also mention these two methods most frequently, but they reverse the order. Economists and political scientists check the receipt of citations from colleagues as the third most frequently used method, whereas sociologists cite their placement on mailing lists of state agencies as third. For sociologists, the receipt of citations from colleagues ties with the checking of newspapers for fifth position. Economists accord fourth place to the receipt of assistance from librarians, whereas political scientists and sociologists mark it sixth. Faculty members in the three disciplines seldom either consult appropriate indexes or draw on the resources of associations and professional societies.

Historians have closer agreement with economists (rho = .73) than with political scientists (rho = .59) and sociologists (rho = .57). At most, however, these relationships may be labeled moderate. Like economists and political scientists, historians draw the most extensively on citations in the general and bibliographic literature of their subject field. However, unlike other social scientists, they list assistance from librarians ahead of the receipt of citations from colleagues. Their placement of state checklists in fourth place suggests a variation in search strategies from those of other social scientists. Perhaps these differences in search strategies can be accounted for by the fact that historians often seek materials of archival, rather than current, nature. To a greater extent, historians seek retrospective information held by state agencies. Therefore, it

Table 4-12   Methods Used for Locating State Publications

Methods Used for Locating State Publications	Discipline				
	Economics	History	Political Science	Sociology	Total
By consulting *Monthly Checklist of State Publications*	3	6	3	3	15
By consulting *Legislative Research Checklist*	2	2	5	2	11
By consulting individual state checklists	4	12	6	6	28
By checking newspapers	7	7	10	26	50
By contacting state agencies	25	11	22	37	95
By drawing on resources of associations	8	5	7	14	34
By drawing on resources of professional societies	2	8	3	17	30
By finding citations in the general literature or special bibliographies in their subejct field	33	34	26	32	125
By being on mailing lists of state agencies	12	3	11	27	53
By receiving citations from colleagues	23	13	13	26	75
By receiving assistance from librarians	15	19	8	18	60
Other	2	2	1	–	5

would seem less likely that state agencies maintain the type of mailing lists that would be useful to the historian. Historians accord a slightly higher position to the category of "drawing on resources of professional societies" than do the other social scientists, listing it sixth, whereas others rank it from seventh to eleventh.

Although frequency of library use and highest degree offered are not significant variables, it should be noted that 80 percent of those faculty members using the *Monthly Checklist of State Publications* are heavy documents users. An examination by institution of the various ways used to locate state publications revealed that none of the social scientists at baccalaureate institutions, public and private, use either the *Monthly Checklist* or the Council of State Government's *Legislative Research Checklist*. Limited support for the other ways was given at baccalaureate institutions.

In general, then, social scientists locate state publications mainly by finding citations in their subject literature, contacting state agencies, and receiving citations from colleagues; the pattern does not differ for interview subjects who consult state publications. Their use, however, primarily relates to research needs.

These social scientists are unfamiliar with the existence of the Library of Congress' *Monthly Checklist of State Publications* or of checklists produced by individual states, including their own. Still, they question the value of listings for other states as their institutional library probably does not have these publications. They suggested that the acquisition of personal copies of publications for their own state is difficult enough without trying to collect selected items for other states.

Municipal Government

As already reported, few of the social scientists surveyed who use documents consulted those of municipal governments (79 or 13.8 percent). Perhaps this small percentage underscores the lack of bibliographic control and unity for these publications.

Table 4-13 depicts the methods used to locate information about the publications of municipal governments. None of the methods used received overwhelming support; responses to the specific categories ranged from five to thirty-four. The *Index to Current Urban Documents,* which was initiated in 1972 by Greenwood Press, was intended to enhance bibliographic control of current municipal publications by pulling together in one place the diverse publishing of various cities for the years since 1971 and to offer customers access to their publications through a microform service. Yet, as responses indicated, few of the social scientists surveyed consult this index. For some reason, historians make the most use of the index. Only one political scientist and one sociologist had consulted the *Index to Current Urban Documents*. Viewed from another perspective, 80 percent of the users of this index are members of doctorate-granting institutions, primarily Southern Illinois University and Northwestern University. It might be noted that analysis of the data by the variables of highest degree offered and institutional control did not produce statistically significant differences.

The "other" category for Table 4-13 received only minimal attention. These faculty members emphasize their reliance on friends in governmental

Table 4-13   Methods for Locating Municipal Publications

Methods for Locating Municipal Publications	Disciplines				
	Economics	History	Political Science	Sociology	Total
Using *Index to Current Urban Documents*	–	3	1	1	5
Consulting individual city checklists	1	3	1	2	7
Checking newspapers	2	2	4	9	17
Contacting municipal agencies	10	3	10	8	31
Being on the mailing lists of municipal agencies	2	–	4	6	12
Drawing on resources of associations	2	1	4	5	12
Drawing on resources of professional societies	1	2	3	1	7
Finding citations in the general literature or special bibliographies in their subject field	10	5	10	9	34
Receiving citations from colleagues	10	6	6	6	28
Receiving assistance from librarians	6	7	4	3	20
Other	1	–	3	1	5

positions, personal contacts with city officials, and "diligent" efforts by graduate assistants. One social scientist felt that he relies on "luck."

The Spearman Rank Order Method, which was applied to the data in the table,[12] indicates moderate to strong agreement between the disciplines of political science and sociology (rho = .82), economics and political science (rho = .93), and economics and sociology (rho = .80). Economists rely most

[12] Given the small number of faculty responses, the proportion of ties for a rank is large. Because of this a correction factor had to be incorporated into the computation of Spearman rho (Siegel, 1956, pp. 206-210).

frequently and equally on the methods of contacting municipal agencies, finding citations in the general and bibliographic literature of their subject field, and receiving citations from colleagues.

For political scientists, two categories were mentioned the most frequently and equally: contacting municipal agencies and finding citations in the general and bibliographic literature of the subject fields. Sociologists also placed two categories in the highest position: checking of newspapers and finding citations in the general and bibliographic literature.

The degree of agreement between history and the other social sciences was moderate to low (economics, rho = .52; political science, rho = .27; and sociology, rho = .28). Of all the relationships examined thus far in this study which involve comparisons of disciplines, this one shows the least agreement. The search patterns of historians for pertinent municipal publications vary significantly from those of scholars in other disciplines. Perhaps the explanation for this phenomenon can be discerned from the distributions of responses in Table 4-13. Historians make the least use of municipal documents, a fact that is evidenced by the small number of responses per category; for historians there was only one frequently mentioned category, receiving assistance from librarians, and it was only specified seven times. The other disciplines had more tied categories, which indicated the importance of several methods for learning about the publications of municipal governments.

Five of the social scientists interviewed (7.4 percent) use municipal publications. In fact, four of them are situated at the same institution and have been recipients of research grants from local government. Their city is one of the mid-sized cities selected for an Urban Observatory, which is a cooperative research program between the city and academic institutions in the surrounding area to address local problems. The program is funded by the U.S. Department of Housing and Urban Development (HUD) and the participating local institutions.[13] Therefore, the four social scientists have had projects funded and published through the Urban Observatory program.

For their research, they draw upon sources such as annual reports of departments, legal notices, and published budgets. Such publications enable them to make internal policy analyses. Three of these social scientists have obtained publications by contacting municipal agencies; however, they find this a time-consuming process. "In some respects," one reported, "it is almost as if we were collecting the data ourselves. The acquisition process was so diffuse and in some cases special requests had to be made for the data to be specially compiled." They would like to have the library assist them by initiating the acquisitions process; "this would save time and effort."

---

[13]The purpose of the Urban Observatory is to encourage cities to apply the expertise of the academic community to their major problems, whether of a policy or applied nature, and to further understanding within academia of the problems and issues confronting the cities.

Another of the social scientists at this institution relies on the documents librarian to locate needed municipal publications. He either asks the librarian to find citations for him or finds citations himself in his subject literature and requests that the librarian obtain these publications for him. Occasionally the librarian forwards citations which he believes the economist may find useful. This social scientist has used Greenwood Press' *Index to Current Urban Documents* but feels that he has missed some pertinent citations. In his opinion, municipal publications contain a wealth of information, but much of this may go unnoticed because a title listing does not adequately convey contents; because of this problem he prefers that the documents librarian conduct the literature search for him. Incidentally, two of the other social scientists were unfamiliar with the *Index to Current Urban Documents*.

The final interview subject at this institution who used municipal publications mentioned that he draws upon publications of the Federal government which deal with urban affairs, the collection of his institutional library, and publications received from the government within his municipality.

Municipal publications were reported used by one interview subject situated at another institution; she peruses the subject literature of political science and notes particular programs operating at the municipal level which are of potential interest to her. She then writes to the agency in charge of the program for any available information. She also draws upon a departmental library collection which contains materials gathered for previous research.

H19   (a) There is no statistically significant difference across discipline or highest degree offered as to the age of the government publications most frequently consulted; (b) the age of the government publications consulted does not vary significantly with the level of government that issued them.

Section 9 of the 1962 Depository Library Act, which provides for discretionary disposal of documents after retention for five years, is testimony to the short life span of the average government publication. Yet, there has been no reported research assessing the accuracy of this limited perception.

Survey subjects were asked to specify how old the government publications are that they consult the most frequently. They were requested to check only one response. As depicted in Table 4-14, 292 documents users (51.1 percent) consult publications no more than three years old, whereas seventy-three, or 12.8 percent, use publications more than ten years old. As might be expected, sixty-four, or 87.7 percent, of the users of older documents are historians. However, twenty-four, or 18.1 percent, of the historians search primarily for materials no more than three years old.

There was no statistically significant difference between the age of documents consulted and highest degree offered by the institution, but a pattern of reliance on current sources was apparent when the age of the documents used was compared to discipline (χ^2 (3,5) = 220.83, $p > .01$) and to the frequency of documents use (χ^2 (2,5) = 33.45, $p > .01$). Except for historians, half the social scientists rely on documents no more than three years old.

Table 4-14   Comparison of Age of Documents Used with Disciplines

| | | Age of Documents | | | | | |
Discipline	Less than a year n (%)	1-3 years n (%)	4-5 years n (%)	6-10 years n (%)	Over 10 years n (%)	No set pattern; age varies n (%)	Totals
Economics	25(17.9)	62(44.3)	6(4.3)	4(2.9)	2(1.4)	41(29.3)	140(25.5)
History	11(8.3)	13(9.8)	2(1.5)	1(0.8)	64(48.1)	42(31.6)	133(23.3)
Political Science	34(25.2)	58(43)	6(4.4)	1(0.7)	3(2.2)	33(24.4)	135(23.6)
Sociology	28(17.2)	61(37.4)	11(6.7)	2(1.2)	4(2.4)	57(35)	163(28.5)
Total	98(17.2)	194(34)	25(4.4)	8(1.4)	73(12.8)	172(30.3)	571

The author further analyzed the variables of discipline, highest degree offered, and institutional control by varying the age options for government publications. If the categories are collapsed to reflect groupings of five years and less, and of six years and more, there is a statistically significant relationship with the disciplines (χ^2 (3,2) = 96.13, $p > .001$). A total of 66.5 percent of the economists consult materials no more than five years old. Some 61.3 percent of the sociologists and 72.6 percent of the political scientists have similar interests. For historians the picture is reversed: 80.5 percent use documents over five years old.

The age of the documents most frequently consulted was compared with level of government producing the documents used. The purpose was to see if similar patterns prevailed across levels of government. A total of 49.6 percent of the users of Federal publications consult documents not over three years of age, whereas 12.7 percent of social scientists want publications more than six years old; 31.3 percent have no set age pattern to the publications sought. At the state level, 48.5 percent of the respondents want publications not over three years of age, whereas material over five years old appeals to only 14.7 percent of the social scientists. However, 28.6 percent of the faculty members have no discernible pattern to their search for information. Current municipal publications appeal to forty-six, or 58.2 percent of the social scientists. Only 9.2 percent of them seek publications more than five years old, while nineteen, or 24.1 percent, have no discernible pattern to the publications sought.

The pattern for use of foreign government publications also reflects an emphasis on current (not over three years old) publications. One hundred, or 50.8 percent, of the social scientists seek current publications, while seventeen, or 8.6 percent, desire historical publications (over 10 years old), and seventy-two, or 36.5 percent, have no discernible pattern to their search.

Half the users of the publications of the United Nations and international organizations also desire current documents (55.2 percent). The majority of the other users have no noticeable pattern for the age of the publications desired (36.3 percent). Social scientists seeking documents from the three remaining categories reflecting four and more years comprise less than 10 percent of the users of the documents of international organizations.

Instead of incorporating the category of "no discernible pattern" into that for "over 10 years old," the author also accorded it a separate position for analysis purposes and collapsed the remaining categories into various combinations. There was then a statistically significant difference between disciplines and the age of the documents consulted (χ^2 (3,2) = 190.92, $p > .001$). Well over half the economists (66.5 percent), the political scientists (72.6 percent), and the sociologists (61.3 percent) seek current (five years old or younger) government publications. Only 19.6 percent of the historians want mainly younger documents, whereas for the other disciplines the percentage of faculty members desiring primarily older documents does not exceed 4.3. For each discipline, the percentage of social scientists having no age preference is substantial. It is 29.3 for economists, 31.6 for historians, 24.4 for political scientists, and 35.0 for sociologists.

A redefinition of "current" (three years old or less) did not significantly alter the picture. There was still a statistically significant relationship between discipline and age of documents consulted (χ^2 (3,2) = 136.77, $p > .001$). Again, over half the social scientists other than historians use current documents. Some 50.4 percent of the historians consult older documents, whereas the percentages for the other disciplines do not exceed 10.3. Of course, the percentages for those faculty members having no age preference did remain constant.

As already reported, 30.3 percent of all questionnaire respondents suggested that there is no set pattern to the age of the government publications they seek. Those interview subjects who checked this category explained that they draw mainly upon current materials, three years old or younger. When they need earlier information, it is primarily for time series, statistical data. Additionally they sometimes consult Congressional hearings, court cases, or material in the serial set. Five of the historians interviewed adhere to this pattern; for supplementary information they consult research libraries in the vicinity or visit archives which have collections pertinent to their research interests. Historians seem to realize that libraries cannot hold all of the source material needed. As a minimum their libraries should have the "basic documents needed such as census publications."

Again, if the publications were issued within the past year, social scientists generally feel that libraries would not have them; therefore they explore other methods of gaining access to them, such as contacting their representatives in Congress. For a publication over one year old, they try their library. If the library does not have the publication, they may seek an alternative source of information or try interlibrary loan, Federal agencies, members of Congress, or another library.

The interview subjects who use municipal publications draw upon materials issued within the last ten years; however, they generally want the most recent ones if they are available. Given the irregular nature of bibliographic control for publications of this level of government, they are willing to take whatever source material is available.

In summary, a sizable percentage of faculty members, regardless of discipline, have no set pattern to the age of publication consulted; percentages range from 29.3 to 35. If the interview findings suggest a trend, it is that those social scientists who checked no set pattern also rely primarily upon recent source material, with the possible exception of census data.

Over half the social scientists (excluding historians) rely on documents of a current nature, whether "current" was defined as three years or younger, or five years or less. Statistical manipulation of the responses to this questionnaire item indicates that inclusion of those faculty members seeking documents less than six years old adds only a very small percentage to the category of "current." This finding suggests that perhaps the requirement that depositories retain documents for at least five years could be relaxed. It would seem that documents, regardless of the level of government issuing them, could be weeded from the collection on a discretionary basis after three years.

> H20   The variables of frequency of library use, discipline, or highest degree offered are not statistically significant factors for determining whether or not a social scientist is currently engaged in, or completed within the past year, a scholarly activity intended for publication which cited a government publication(s) in the bibliography or footnotes.

The chi square test indicates that the null hypothesis can be rejected. There is a statistically significant relationship between the citing of documents in a scholarly writing and the frequency of documents use (χ^2 (3,1) = 179.90, $p > .001$). Eighty-seven percent of the heavy users cite documents, and 70.4 percent of the moderate users do also. On the other hand, limited users are almost evenly divided as to whether they do (50.5 percent) or do not (49.5 percent). Non-users overwhelmingly have not cited documents (85.5 percent). This finding confirms the earlier one that there is a statistically significant difference between heavy and moderate users, and limited users and non-users, thereby lending support to the groupings used.

There was also a statistically significant difference with the variable of discipline (χ^2 (3,1) = 20.48, $p > .001$). Over half of the economists (67.8 percent), political scientists (68.7 percent), and sociologists (64.5 percent) cite documents, whereas historians are almost evenly split as to whether they do (48.5 percent) or do not (51.5 percent).

Chi square analysis was also applied to highest degree offered and institutional control, but significant differences emerged only for highest degree offered (χ^2 (3,1) = 18.29, $p > .001$). Approximately half the faculty members at baccalaureate (45.1 percent) and master's-level (53.6 percent) institutions cite documents, whereas the split at doctorate-granting institutions is more divergent. Two-thirds of these faculty members (67.5 percent) cite documents whereas only one-third (32.5 percent) do not.

Examination of responses per institution indicates an even distribution at all of the institutions except four. At three of these, doctorate-granting institutions (Indiana University, Bloomington; Michigan State University; and Northwestern University), approximately three-fourths of the faculty members cite documents in their scholarly writing. At the fourth institution, a master's-level institution, the situation is reversed: only 27.8 percent of the social scientists there include documents.

> H21   A majority of faculty members are unaware of the variety of programs librarians use to promote awareness of government publications.

Faculty members were asked to check those methods which they thought the library staff employ to enhance awareness of important government publications. Approximately half of them (302, or 44.21 percent) suggested that there is no regular program in their libraries or that they have no idea what is offered. These social scientists are evenly distributed as to frequency of libary use, highest degree offered, and institutional control.

Although the other faculty members cite method(s), one-fourth of them admitted that they were either guessing or checking only those few options about which they were certain. The methods most frequently checked are: tours (202), entrance of documents into the public card catalog (158), maintenance of browsing areas (128) and of displays (113), preparation of bibliographic guides to specific disciplines (107), preparation of manuals and handouts (97), brochures (95), and library lectures conducted through the classroom (91).

Librarians at each institution were queried regarding whether they have regular programs for informing faculty members and students of important documents; if there are such programs, librarians were asked to specify the methods employed. The responses were compared with those of the faculty members in an attempt to determine the accuracy of faculty perceptions. The results of the comparison are presented in Chapter 5, which relates the findings of the library questionnaires.

> H22   There is no statistically significant difference across discipline, highest degree offered, institution, or frequency of documents use as to the means by which faculty members make students aware of the government publications collection at the university or college library.

All the social scientists surveyed, regardless of whether they are documents users or not, were asked to respond to a query as to whether or not they make their students aware of the documents collection housed in the library. About a fourth of them (193, or 28.3 percent) have never had occasion to mention the collection to students. The rest of the faculty marked one or more of the remaining categories. The two most frequently checked categories show faculty preference for the informal methods of suggesting the collection as a valuable source of information (301) and of referring students to a library (228). Only seventy-three social scientists had invited a librarian to provide specialized instruction on the use of the library, but 225 faculty members formally promote the collection through specific class assignments.

One hundred fifty-seven responding faculty members include documents on required or suggested reading lists. For example, two of them had assigned the *U.S. Government Manual* as a required textbook. One of the economists who had used documents as required reading in his public finance course wrote a letter which he attached to the completed questionnaire. He wanted to share the following experience:

> I tried to use a particular government document, *Special Analysis of the United States Budget,* as a text, but consider my problems. As I was unable to order a supply for the students before the semester began, I had to arrange my lectures so as to allow five weeks before the document could be used. During this time period, the class was supposed to write the GPO for copies. When they did write and submit

checks, the document was in some instances not in stock and had to be sought from a different office, or the wrong document was sent to them. In sum there is simply no merchandising system geared to the needs of users.

Another social scientist who had required readings in documents has written an article on the value of documents for teaching public administration. In his opinion documents provide students with a notion of the climate in which administrative decision making takes place and of how governments operate. He encourages instructors to have their students work with the source material issued by governments and held by libraries (Stein, 1975, 98-105).

As the categories presented in the questionnaire item were not mutually exclusive, and as respondents could check more than one category, chi square analysis was not applied. Examiniation of the data on the basis of frequency distributions did reveal certain trends. A much larger percentage of heavy and moderate users of documents encourage student awareness by formal and informal means (the percentage range was from 68.8 to 84.1) than do limited users and non-users. Heavy users account for half of those who include documents on required or suggested reading lists (52.9 percent), whereas moderate users comprise one-third (31.2 percent) of the remaining social scientists in this group.

Comparison of the data to the level of government issuing the documents used did not produce notable differences for municipal government except in two categories. Seventy percent of the social scientists using municipal publications enhance student awareness of them by informally suggesting the collection as a valuable source of information, whereas only 12.7 percent of them ask librarians to provide specialized instruction in the use of the library.

To summarize questionnaire findings, frequency of documents use was the only variable giving notable differences and challenging the null hypothesis. Of the faculty members consulting documents for resources that might be of value to their students, the majority make students aware of documents by informal means—suggesting the collection as a valuable source of information or referring students to a library.

During the interviews, some of the social scientists described the ways in which they assign government publications for particular class purposes. The purpose of this section is not to quantify individual methods or to describe all the methods mentioned; instead it suggests some of the ways in which government publications are being used and some of the problems encountered by students in using these sources.

Twenty-five, or 48.1 percent, of the fifty-two social scientists who described use of government publications by their classes related that their students experience problems: the students may be encountering government publications for the first time and easily become "overwhelmed" by the amount of material available and by the library's treatment of these publications. Government publications are difficult to browse through, and the Superintendent of

Documents (SUDOC) system appears "illogical" to them. At best it is a system which students have not previously encountered. They become "easily discouraged by the complexity of the documents department and by its organization." They also become "frustrated by the fact that the main card catalog did not provide a complete listing of documents holdings." Finally the social scientists mentioned that students are reluctant to request assistance. They do not want to disturb librarians, who appear preoccupied with other duties, and they are hesitant to approach the same librarian twice. Reasons given included that librarians show impatience when asked for assistance and that students do not want to expose their lack of ability to maneuver through the documents collection. Social scientists sometimes refer students to specific librarians, but problems occasionally arise when that person is not available and the librarian who accepts the question lacks expertise with the publications of that level of government. Perhaps these comments made by the social scientists indicate a greater reluctance among students than among faculty members to request assistance from library staff members. At any rate, student use of government publications merits investigation.

Many social scientists explained that their use of government publications is unsystematic. They do not feel that they are sophisticated users of the government publications collection, and they find that they are imparting the same habits to their students. As one political scientist put it, "I show them what has worked the best for me."

In many cases, students are not expected to do an extensive search of government publications. For one American history class, students had to search the *Congressional Globe,* the same source which the instructor uses most frequently for his research.

A political scientist whose teaching area comprises foreign policy had his students use the *Daily Reports* (Foreign Broadcast and Information Service), Congressional hearings and committee prints, and selected United Nations publications such as the *UN Monthly Chronicle.* Although he is not presently involved in research, he obtains current information for teaching from the *Daily Reports,* public announcements of the State Department, and national newspapers. Similarly another political scientist receives public announcements on contemporary policy issues and clips those relating to his class needs. The clipping files are retained in his office for a year or two, and students draw upon them for class projects. He finds that the library's collection of resources on these topics is seldom as current as are his clipping files.

One sociologist uses government publications for teaching and has a graduate assistant locate specific pieces of data and record the sources from which the data are gathered. This way new graduate assistants need only to ask the library staff members for the location of specific titles. Another sociologist covers demography in his introductory course and wants his students to realize the wealth of information contained in government publications. He therefore assigns each student a particular state and expects him to answer a set of questions such as the median income for the years 1960 and 1970. There is no set pattern to the time periods covered by the questions. It really depends on a "whim of the moment"; he does vary the years each semester so that students will not pass along the pool of questions and answers!

Economists emphasized that in order to test hypotheses, students need to draw upon current statistical data, much of which is produced by the Federal government; must know basic documents reference sources; and must know how governmental agencies collect data. One economist even instructs students in how to order personal copies, such as reports issued by the National Technical Information Service (NTIS).

One department of sociology offered a field project in a nearby city. For credit, graduate students participated in several aspects of survey research and learned about questionnaire construction, sampling, interviewing, coding, data analysis, and report writing. As some of the data used is collected and distributed by the Federal government, students thus discover the role that government publications can play in social science research.

As is evident from the few examples given, social scientists find government publications an asset to teaching. Three sociologists summarized the role of government information for their professional needs as follows: These publications provide background information and illustrations for teaching, updated monographs and textbooks for teaching, and constitute a primary resource for research.

> H23   Faculty members, regardless of the extent of their documents use, the method by which they learned to find government publications, discipline, or highest degree offered, do not differ significantly in their preference as to the means by which library staff members instruct students about government publications.

The null hypothesis cannot be rejected. One-half of the respondents (350 faculty, or 51.2 percent) specified instruction through library class lectures, tours, term paper clinics, or reference rap sessions as the method of instruction that they prefer the library to use in assisting students in the use of documents. Other instructional methods mentioned were formal credit courses (29), formal noncredit courses (47), and incorporation of instruction into existing subject bibliographic courses (50). Respondents to the "other" category hold the opinion that instruction can best be handled through question negotiation between the user and the librarian during the normal reference interview process. Seventy-two, or 10.5 percent, of the social scientists believe that no instruction is required, while another 104, or 15.2 percent, hold no opinion on the subject. One social scientist who did not express an opinion explained that he is "ambivalent on the value of instruction unless it could be directly related to student interests and needs." He believes that students only remember the information presented if they have to use it for a research project.

Chi square analysis did not produce statistically different findings in relation to the variables of frequency of documents use, institutional control, discipline, the method by which faculty members learn to use the documents collection, the age of documents consulted, and highest degree offered by the institution. Even those faculty members who learned to find materials through a trial-and-error process or formal course work emphasized the same approach—instruction through programs such as library class lectures and tours.

Validity and Reliability of Findings

Pretesting the faculty questionnaire suggested unclear situations and provided criticism of question phraseology. On the basis of comments made by social scientists, the questionnaire was revised and shortened. Interviews offered another indication of how social scientists interpreted selected questionnaire items. A secondary purpose of interviewing was to provide validity and reliability checks on questionnaire findings. This section of the chapter reports first on validity.

During the interviews, there was a brief discussion of social scientists' definition of government publications. They view these publications as informational matter not restricted to the items disseminated by the Government Printing Office. This definition takes into account ephemera and is similar to that presented on page two of the faculty questionnaire.[14] Interview subjects also experienced no difficulties with the term "search systems," and related their reasons for using or not using computerized search systems. The social scientists interviewed consult Public Use Tapes but not the Census Summary Tapes, because they need "samples of individual records rather than summary data."

Only one-third of the nonrespondents do not use government publications at all; they view these publications as informational matter but offered various reasons for not using them. For example, two of the nonrespondents had used government publications "years ago" when they researched public policy. They are now more concerned with theory.

Those nonrespondents who use government publications, as well as the other interview subjects, supplied titles of selected government documents which they consult. During forty-five interviews, the investigator noticed copies of documents in faculty offices and/or the social scientists pointed out documents which they had received from government bodies; these included ephemera, public announcements, and press releases of Federal executive departments and Congressional committees. Some of the documents in their offices were borrowed from their institutional libraries. Moreover these forty-five social scientists

[14] A government publication was defined as informational matter which has been published as an individual document at government expense or as required by law.

represented heavy, moderate, and limited users of their libraries' documents collections.

Other indicators of validity were that documents users are familiar with the publishing records of certain executive agencies and Congressional committees. They detailed their search strategies for locating different types of government publications and provided examples for clarification and illustration. Over half the interview subjects volunteered the name of a documents librarian and commented on their association with that individual. One department distributes a list of "Major Reference Sources in Economics" to all students specializing in the discipline. The handout contains forty-three citations, twenty-seven of which are to government publications. Also, seven interview subjects showed copies of their dissertations, articles, or books in which government documents were cited.

Twenty interview subjects (heavy, moderate, and limited users of government publications) asked questions of the author. For example, nine wanted to know sources which might be of value to immediate research interests. Ten volunteered that their institutional libraries are Federal depositories, but they were "curious" about how their libraries decide which publications to receive. Six of the twenty interview subjects were interested to learn that the author teaches a graduate-level course on government publications. As one social scientist explained, "given the proliferation of source material and the problems involved in locating documents relevant to my needs, I can see the value of a course devoted entirely to government publications. In fact, I wish that I had the time to take such a course myself." Also seven social scientists "welcomed" a library-related study of government publications, hoping that the findings would be widely disseminated to library administrators who might be able to improve and "simplify" access to the documents held within their collections and to increase bibliographic control over the machine-readable data files belonging to other departments on campus.

A nonbiased selection of interview subjects also contributes to validity. For those disciplines with more than three social scientists, interview subjects were selected on the basis of frequency of documents use and questionnaire responses for which additional information was desired.

The following six categories provided the basis for the interviews and constituted checks on reliability: (1) frequency of documents use, (2) use or non-use of data bases, (3) use or non-use of indexes, (4) the levels of governments for which publications were used, (5) age of documents used, and (6) methods for locating needed government publications and information. The responses given during the interviews were then compared to those of the questionnaire in order to determine consistency of responses over time. Nonrespondents were not analyzed.

The fifty-three social scientists responded identically on questionnaires and in the interviews for all categories except one, frequency of documents use. Two moderate users marked on their questionnaire that they had used the documents collection "6 to 10" times the previous year, but mentioned use of "11 to 15" times during the interviews; this variation was too slight to alter findings; moderate users were defined as those consulting the collection between six and fifteen times. There were no variations in responses for heavy or limited users, as well as non-users.

Seven interview subjects indicated on the questionnaire that there was no discernible pattern as to the age of the government publications which they consulted. They explained that their response reflected the fact that they rely heavily on current publications (no more than three years of age), but that they also often use retrospective statistical data.

Finally, social scientists who did not suggest on the questionnaires that they browse or use the public card catalog or indexes to locate documents were queried about the value of these methods in meeting their information requirements. They consistently responded that these methods are "haphazard," "inefficient," and "prolonged the search" because they are "low yield" or seldom lead to the desired publications. In summary, the interviews confirmed the validity and reliability of the present investigation.

SUMMARY

This chapter reports the results of the analysis of the data collected through faculty questionnaire and interviews. The analysis was presented in two main sections. The first provided general descriptive data about the mix of faculty involvement with teaching, research, and administrative duties; about their association with research, sponsored and nonsponsored; and about faculty estimations of their use of the library and documents collections during the previous year. The second section examined the findings in relation to the hypotheses stated in Chapter 1.

The questionnaire probed the reasons for use and non-use in general terms. Analysis of the data in terms of the hypotheses disclosed certain questions and areas which could be explored in more depth through interviewing. For example, there could be a probe of search strategies, which would reveal the extent and importance of browsing; there could also be an examination of faculty awareness of computerized search systems and the financial sources for faculty members using fee-for-service searches. The major reason reported for infrequent use and non-use of documents was that governments publish little or nothing of value to an immediate field, yet this perception is general and does not give a full understanding of the nature of source material available to social scientists in their specialty fields. The Federal government has produced an extensive literature of value to the study of American history, but of undoubtedly more value in some special fields of history than in others.

Frequency of faculty use of the library's documents collection is not a good indicator of the use by faculty members of government publications in general. Limited users and non-users of the documents collection may, in fact, receive government documents through other channels. The major reason for non-use of government publications, as already indicated, is that faculty members perceive that governments publish little or nothing of value to their immediate fields. Yet an important secondary reason is that the amount of time spent in searching for documents is out of proportion to what is found. This finding suggests that faculty members may be influenced by two factors: perceived quality and ease of access. Through a variety of means, librarians could show social scientists that particular information exists and is available in the library, but this neither means that the materials will be used nor does it fully address the issue of ease of access to publications which might be housed in separate collections arranged by a special classification system (SUDOC) and made accessible through means other than the public card catalog.

The investigation disclosed few statistically significant differences among disciplines. It did show, in general, that economists are the heaviest users of government publications. There are great similarities between use of documents by faculty members in economics and political science, except that those in the latter discipline seek documents more for current events and issues of interest. Sociologists have similar patterns of use, but they make greater use of the public card catalog for locating documents held by the library and are the heaviest users of data bases, in particular of the census tapes.

Historians are the divergent group, although the differences are not always statistically significant. They are predominantly limited users and non-users of documents, who consult documents primarily for historical information and who use older documents. They make limited use of municipal publications and differ from the other social scientists in the means used to locate municipal and state publications but not Federal publications. Perhaps this can be explained on the basis of the age of the material sought and of the current state of bibliographic control for the publishing of different levels of government.

Interviewing enabled the author to supplement questionnaire findings and to probe the means by which social scientists gain access to information needed to fulfill their professional responsibilities. Two of the six interview sites constituted "maverick" institutions where the faculty members exhibited characteristics different from their counterparts at schools with the same control and degree programs. At the first institution most of the faculty members in the four disciplines under study completed questionnaires, and, moreover, they all use government publications at least to some extent. Interviewing disclosed that seniors at this undergraduate institution have to complete a research paper in their major subject discipline. Social scientists therefore have to be alert to topics for which government publications might be beneficial. Given student unfamiliarity with the library's treatment of government publications, it is not uncommon for them to assist students and to join with the documents librarian in the search for source materials. The social scientists pointed out that as students cannot always schedule their visits to the library during times when the librarian is on duty, they easily become frustrated by the information overload of government publications and by the arrangement of the documents collection.

The other "maverick" institution was selected because of local government sponsorship of faculty research and social scientist use of data bases. It was found that the research is conducted through an Urban Observatory, a program designed to increase cooperation between the academic community and the local government on major urban problems.[15] None of the other academic institutions surveyed are affiliated with Urban Observatories. The use of data bases by social scientists at this school is related to faculty research interests and reflects a need for unpublished statistical data. The magnetic tapes, which are purchased personally or from departmental fundings and/or research grants, are retained within the department for the use of faculty members within that discipline.

The section on validity and reliability indicated a close correspondence between interview comments and questionnaire responses. Government publications play a part in meeting the information requirements of many social scientists. Moreover their use of government publications is not confined to printed sources or to the documents disseminated by the Government Printing Office.

Although only a small number of nonrespondents to the questionnaire were interviewed, the assumption that nonrespondents constitute non-users of the documents collection can be questioned. Nonrespondents were not confined to non-users, but they also included heavy, moderate, and limited users.

The assumption of documents librarians that government publications constitute an underutilized library resource apparently has some validity. Social scientists do not always rely on those government publications housed in the library, partially because some libraries are not collecting publications soon enough after their public release. Such libraries need to determine ways in which they can more speedily acquire and process new government publications.

The comments of one sociologist, situated at a doctorate-granting and research institution, emphasized that government publications constitute an important resource for social scientists. He indicated that his department could not easily recruit new faculty members if the library did not have a strong

---

[15]City officials select topics to be studied from among designated urban priorities. Members of academic institutions then submit proposals in these areas, and a Policy Board, consisting of representatives from the city government and the participating colleges and universities, decides which proposals to fund. Project results are disseminated locally to city officials, appropriate community institutions, interested citizens, and other interested governmental bodies and organizations.

collection of government publications, particularly those containing statistical data. The reason is that sociologists are turning more than they formerly did to quantitative techniques and empirical analysis in their research.

As reflected by the interviews, the use of government publications by social scientists is *not* broadly based. They are more likely to rely on the resources of selected executive departments and agencies and Congressional committees; they also rely upon certain *specific types* of publications. These findings suggest that perhaps a core collection for government publications could be constructed.

Most of the social scientists interviewed regard librarians as resource people who are familiar with their libraries' collections and with methods for obtaining information contained in other libraries. They see librarians as performing a "time-saving function" by searching indexes and guides for them. Librarians are seen as more efficient than are the social scientists themselves in conducting literature searches. Evidently the amount of time expended in searching for needed publications is a barrier to use; libraries therefore need to devise strategies to ease access to the major publications they hold.

The subject literature for specific disciplines constitutes the prime means of awareness for the more important publications. The assumption of some social scientists is that the monographic and periodical literature eventually reflects the major government publications of their disciplines. Perhaps librarians need to test the accuracy of this perception, especially since delays of months or years can be expected in references to journal and monographic literature. Given the unsystematic nature of the literature search strategies for many social scientists, it is possible that these individuals cannot handle the volume of government publication or differentiate between the relevant and irrelevant. Furthermore, documents collections may be cluttered with trivial, unnecessary, and redundant publications. Perhaps part of the problem is that there is an absence of quality control for what governments publish.

Finally the interviews showed that librarians need to be aware of user needs and problems encountered in the use of the government publications collection. Such awareness can pinpoint areas of dissatisfaction with the quality of the reference service provided and can also lead to an opportunity for faculty members to participate in collection building. Five of the social scientists interviewed wished that librarians would ask their advice on acquisitions of government publications. One economist, for example, mentioned that his library carries the *Statistics of Publicly Owned Electric Utilities in the United States* (Federal Power Commission). He suspects that he may be the only user of this annual series. However, the library does not own the publication over time. As there are gaps in the holdings, he can only compare data for specific years by supplementing the library's collection with personal copies and with the holdings of another depository library.

5. Library Study Results

In order to place questionnaire responses from social science faculty members in proper context, this cross-institutional study overviewed the government publications collections at the seventeen libraries surveyed. In particular, the study examined the general acquisition, classification, arrangement, and servicing of these publications. The insights gained from a comparison of faculty use patterns and perceptions to library practices should enable academic libraries to better structure their organization and service programs for documents in the best interest of their clientele, present and potential.

This chapter, based on the questionaire completed by the persons in charge of the documents collections,[1] is divided into two sections. The first section provides descriptive information about the documents collections at the seventeen libraries under investigation. It examines the libraries as a composite and by groupings sharing similar institutional control and highest degree offered. The second section analyzes the library hypotheses presented in Chapter 1 and focuses on the variable of frequency of documents use.

For the purposes of statistical analysis, the .05 of significance was used again. The chi square test, which was utilized through the Statistical Package for the Social Sciences (SPSS), enabled the investigator to determine if a significant relationship existed among selected variables. Relationships lacking statistical significance were also identified, and certain of them are presented in the body of this chapter.

[1] Appendix F contains the library questionnaire.

DESCRIPTIVE CHARACTERTISTICS OF
THE LIBRARIES

The first item on the questionnaire asked if the library staff had undertaken studies of faculty use of the government publications collection. Only two of the libraries, Northwestern University and Case Western Reserve University, responded in the affirmative. Both of these studies are discussed in Chapter 2. However, it should be noted that both of these studies were conducted more than eight years ago and that no formal follow-up investigations have been undertaken. Comparisons between these two studies and the present one are presented in Chapter 6.

Depository Status for Non-Government Printing Office (GPO) Publications

The seventeen libraries under investigation may be receiving, as official depositories, more documents produced by the United States government than those offered solely by the Superintendent of Documents. Operating on this assumption, the investigator asked the librarians if their libraries have been designated as official depositories for the publications of any other Federal departments or agencies. Eight libraries indicated that they have been. These libraries represent public master's-level (1), public doctorate-granting (3), private baccalaureate (2), private master's-level (1), and private doctorate-granting (1) institutions.

Seven of these libraries receive maps produced by the U.S. Geological Survey, and one is a recipient of the *Comprehensive Planning (701) Reports* produced by the Department of Housing and Urban Development. Two of the depositories for the U.S. Geological Survey also receive documents from other Federal agencies, either the Defense Mapping Agency or the Department of Labor, Regional Office.

Collection of Nonfederal Publications

Four questionnaire items probed whether or not the libraries systematically collect the publications of state governments, municipal governments, governments of foreign countries, or the United Nations and other international organizations. Four, or 23.5 percent, of the libraries (all from private institutions offering degree programs no higher than the master's) do not systematically collect documents except from the Federal level of government.

Eleven of the seventeen libraries (64.7 percent) systematically collect state publications, however. The six exceptions, all private institutions, are evenly distributed according to highest degree offered. Further analysis of these eleven libraries disclosed that they all collect publications from their own states. For eight of the libraries, these publications are received as part of official depository programs.

Approximately one-half of the libraries collecting state publications (five, or 45.5 percent) also gather publications from other states in the region. Of these, two are parts of doctorate-granting institutions and another two are associated with master's-level institutions. The final library is at a public baccalaureate institution.

Only two of the five libraries, representing doctorate-granting and baccalaureate institutions, gather publications from selected states in other geographical regions. It should be stated that the aforementioned baccalaureate institution collects only selected items from state governments. Presumably the library from the doctorate-granting institution gathers a broader range of publications. Finally, one library (from a private, doctorate-granting institution) collects selected government publications from every state in the union.

Interestingly, the publications of the United Nations and other international organizations are collected as frequently as are those of state governments. Eleven libraries collect documents produced by international organizations. Five of the libraries not systematically gathering these publications are associated with private institutions offering degree programs no higher than the master's and one is part of a public master's level institution. Given the focus of this investigation on the publications generated within the United States, no attempt was made to determine either the specific subject areas or the international organizations whose materials are collected.

Few of the libraries surveyed collect publications from municipal and foreign governments. Approximately one-third of the libraries (five, or 29.4 percent) collect municipal publications. These libraries are predominantly located at doctorate-granting and research institutions (3). (However, there is one from a private master's-level institution and another from a public baccalaureate instituion.)

All five libraries collect, to varying degrees, the publications of their own municipality. Only two of them gather municipal documents on a broader geographical basis. These libraries, which represent doctoral and research institutions, acquire publications from other cities in their respective states and from selected cities throughout the nation.

Publications of foreign governments are collected least often. Less than a fourth of the libraries (four, or 23.5 percent) gather these publications. These libraries are all associated with public institutions offering graduate degrees.

Participation in Consortia

To conclude a discussion of the levels of government from which documents are collected at this point might produce a misleading impression. Libraries have an alternative and supplement to the acquisition of expensive and seldom used research materials. They can participate in a cooperative depository or consortium such as the Center for Research Libraries. For a fee, a library can join the Center, a nonprofit organization located in Chicago, and borrow government publications from it as needed—in particular those of state and municipal governments. Since January 1952 the Center has collected regularly, and as comprehensively as possible, all state documents, excluding session laws and compiled statistics; agricultural experiment station publications have been collected selectively; and there is also a selective collection of pre-1952 state documents. The advantage of this operation is that libraries are able to maintain selective in-house collections of state documents and borrow less needed documents from the Center.

Because of the existence of cooperative depositories or consortia, the author asked if the libraries supplement their holdings of government publications through such arrangements. Seven, or 41.2 percent, of the respondents answered in the affirmative. Their libraries, with two exceptions, are associated with doctorate-granting institutions. In fact, only one of the doctoral institutions, Case Western Reserve University, does not participate in such arrangements. The two exceptions are parts of public institutions—one master's-level and the other baccalaureate. At the one baccalaureate institution, Indiana University, Kokomo, the library has access to documents through the Indiana Univeristy Regional Campus Libraries System.

The seven participating libraries were analyzed to determine if they systematically collect documents from other levels of government or if they rely solely on cooperative arrangements for such materials. The University of Notre Dame Library is the least likely to acquire nonfederal publications. That library is a depository for publications of the European Economic Community, but it relies on the Center for Research Libraries to provide other needed government publications.

Collection Arrangement and Classification Schemes

Certain policies and practices of the library may encourage or inhibit use of government publications. For example, some depository libraries segregate their government publications from other library resources and centralize the acquisition, reference, and cataloging functions into one separate department, whereas other libraries keep some of these functions within departments that handle materials of other publishers. Other libraries treat government publications like the rest of the library's holdings, entering them into the general collection and using the card catalog as the primary means of access. Finally, some libraries merge these two approaches by placing some of the documents together in separate areas of the library with their own classification schemes, the remainder of the documents, in particular periodicals and reference works, are merged with the rest of the library's materials.

Of the libraries under study, six keep all their United States documents in separate collections, whereas one incorporates all of its documents into the general collection. The remaining ten libraries separate some of the publications and integrate the rest with the general collection. For five of these libraries, some government publications are also incorporated into pamphlet files.

Regarding the classification system employed, fifteen of the libraries arrange their United States publications, in part or entirely, according to the Superintendent of Documents Classification scheme (SUDOC). Six of these libraries employ only the SUDOC scheme, while the others also use the Library of Congress or Dewey systems for publications located in the general collection. Only two libraries do not use the SUDOC method. At one of them, all the documents are arranged in the general collection under Library of Congress numbers, while at the other the documents contained in the separate collection are alphabetically arranged by agency.

Due to the mixture of collection arrangements, the author could not make extensive comparisons between the users of separate and integrated collections. However, insights can be provided into user perceptions of separate collections. A cautionary note, however, might be inserted. It would be difficult, for a study of merged collections, to separate the use of government publications from the use of other library holdings. Such an examination might show how effectively documents are used in conjunction with conventional library resources, but an investigator would have to build this comparison into the research design of the study.

The libraries under examination show more variation in their organization and classification of state and municipal publications than they do with Federal publications. One library incorporates its state publications into the general collection, whereas another places them in a pamphlet file and two others keep all of them in separate collections. The remaining libraries use combinations of these two approaches. State publications are arranged alphabetically or by Dewey, Library of Congress, agencies, or state library schemes.

Similar patterns are evident in the handling of municipal publications. They are found in pamphlet files, separate and/or general collections, or combinations of the three. Similarly, a variety of classification schemes are employed.

Percentages of Government Publications Received

In addition to the areas already mentioned, the author sought information on the percentage of Federal document categories received, the listing of documents into the public card catalog, and the number of staff members servicing the documents collection.

The librarians in charge of the collections were asked to estimate the percentage of Federal document categories received from the Superintendent of Documents, and were given seven options from which to choose. As Table 5.1 indicates, four of the respondents suggested that their libraries select over 90 percent, but eight of them (47 percent) estimated that their libraries take less than 50 percent of the available categories. These libraries are all with bacca- laureate institutions, private and public, or with public (Eastern Illinois Univer- sity) and private (Butler University and John Carroll University) master's-level institutions. Valparaiso University is the only school in the range of 50 to 69 percent, while the libraries at the public doctorate institutions and at North- western University account for those receiving over 90 percent. The category of 70 to 89 percent includes Central Michigan University and the remaining two private doctorate institutions (Case Western Reserve University and the University of Notre Dame).

Entrance of Documents in Card Catalog

Given the distribution of responses for the percentages of categories received, the next questionnaire item related to whether or not any cards for government publications were placed in the public card catalog. Fifteen, or 88.2 percent, of the respondents reported that their libraries do enter documents into their card catalogs, but to varying degrees. Only two libraries, representing public master's- level and private baccalaureate institutions, do not enter documents in the card catalog.

As depicted in Table 5-2, only one library, the same library that integrates all its Federal publications into the general collection, has extensive access to its documents from the card catalog. For all the other libraries, less than 50 percent of the documents held are available in the card catalog.[2] This fact underscores

Table 5-1   Estimated Percentage of Depository
Categories Received

Percentage Received	Number	Percent	Cumulative Frequency (Percentage)
Over 90	4	23.5	100.0
70-89	3	17.6	76.4
50-69	1	5.9	58.8
30-49	4	23.5	52.9
10-29	4	23.5	29.4
Unspecified	1	5.9	5.9

[2] It might be noted that the library at one of the private Master's institutions is pre- paring a public card file for all of its documents series, current and retrospective. Cards for government periodicals are already entered in the card file.

the unreliability of the card catalog as a primary source for accessing the majority of the documents holdings of academic depostiory libraries.

Of the eleven libraries collecting state publications, only seven enter them in the public card catalog. One library at a public doctorate-granting institution catalogs over 90 percent of its state publications, whereas the other six place less than 10 percent in the card catalog. As for the five libraries gathering municipal publications, one does not enter them in the card catalog and the other three catalog less than 10 percent. Finally, the library at the same public doctorate-granting institution just mentioned catalogs over 90 percent of its municipal publications.

Documents Staff Size

Because the ability of librarians to provide reference service and to engage in outreach activities is partially dependent on staff size, the author asked for the number of FTE staff members servicing documents. The total number ranged from one person with a part-time assignment to thirteen employees; the median was 2.9 and the mean was 3.8. The five libraries having over four documents-related staff members are in institutions with graduate programs, primarily those offering the doctorate.

An attempt was made to differentiate among the several types of personnel assigned to work with government publications. That is, respondents were asked to specify the number of librarians, clerks, and paraprofessional personnel involved with documents. The number of librarians varies from fewer than one (part-time responsibilities for government publications) to seven; however, the mean is 1.6 and the median is 1.1. Approximately two-thirds of the depositories (eleven, or 64.7 percent) reported that they have one or less professional staff member assigned to the servicing of government publications. There is no dis-

Table 5-2   Comparison of Percentage of Federal Documents Received with the Percentage of Documents Entered in the Public Card Catalog

| Percentage of Documents Received | Percentage Entered in Card Catalog | | | | |
	Over 90	49-30	29-10	Under 10	Unspecified
Over 90			2	2	
89-70		1	1		1
69-50				1	
49-30			2	2	
29-10	1		1	1	1
Unspecified				1	
Total	1	1	6	7	2

tinct pattern as to institutional control or highest degree offered. Master's-level institutions do not necessarily have larger documents staffs than do baccalaureate institutions.

Ten of the libraries stated that they have one clerical employee assigned to work with government publications; three libraries responded that they have two clerks; two reported having clerical assistance only on part-time bases; and two have no such employee category. Eight of the depositories have no paraprofessional assistance, while paraprofessional staff at two of the libraries have part-time documents assignments. The sizes of documents staffs at other libraries range from one to four paraprofessionals; at thirteen, or 76.5 percent, of the libraries, reference librarians also service the government publications collections. The four exceptions are two public master's-level and two doctorate-granting (one public and the other private) institutions having total staff sizes ranging from two to five employees. All have a minimum of one professional assigned to servicing government publications.

Comparison of staff size to the variables of highest degree offered, institutional control, and percentage of Federal publications categories received did not produce statistically significant differences. However, comments made by two of the respondents suggest that staff size and personnel problems adversely affect the documents programs. One librarian noted that "our reference function continues to suffer both because of our physical set-up and because we are forced to rely on civil service and student help in this supposedly professional field." Another librarian explained that:

> The fiscal year of 1976-77 cannot be termed as a year of great strides, but rather a year of holding-our-own. Little increase in personnel or available time of the librarian has accounted for this lack of significant progress.

> The personnel of the department were newly hired and thus had to be trained. This training was somewhat complicated due to the work assigned being inappropriate for the temperament, ability and interest of the person. Therefore much time was expended to train and fully develop the Library Clerk. Now the assistant is a committed, useful and valuable addition to the library staff. This can be considered the major accomplishment of the year.

These comments were made at the institution in which 17.1 percent of the forty-one faculty members who expressed reluctance to ask library staff for assistance reside (see H8 of Chapter 4).

HYPOTHESES

This section analyzes the library-related hypotheses, builds upon the descriptive overview already presented in this chapter, and brings out questionnaire items not already discussed.

Since the library hypotheses have had only limited testing in previous research, they might more precisely be labeled as assumptions. Certain of their basic qualities indicate that librarians have gathered little scientific data comparing documents use to long-held library practices and conventions. Perhaps an explanatory note should be inserted. Some items on the library questionnaire were not asked of the social scientists and therefore describe an area only in very general terms. For example, the library questionnaire asked if government publications circulate to faculty members; however, a comparison of circulation to use does not suggest the full impact of library policies on users. These hypotheses merit further investigation.

> H1   The academic library collects, or has access to, the publications from the different levels of government needed and used by its faculty.

The publications of the Federal government receive the most extensive use. They are consulted by the majority of documents users at each institution. Use of the publications of other levels of government, however, is not as widespread, and these publications are not systematically collected by all of the libraries under study.

Eleven of the libraries systematically gather state publications, but use of these publications is not confined to the eleven institutions. Forty-four social scientists from the six remaining institutions, all private, make some use of state publications. Half of these users are associated with two doctorate-granting institutions, one of which comprises a "research" institution as defined by the Carnegie Commission on Higher Education, (Carnegie Commission on Higher Education, 1973, pp. 1-2) while sixteen are associated with master's-level institutions. The final six faculty members are situated in baccalaureate institutions.

Fifty-four, or 68.4 percent, of the users of municipal government publications teach at institutions in which the libraries do not systematically collect municipal publications. The number of faculty members polled per institution ranged from one to twelve, with approximately 75 percent of them clustering at doctorate-granting and public master's-level institutions. However, two of these doctorate-granting institutions comprise "research" institutions as defined by the Carnegie Commission on Higher Education. At one of the private baccalaureate institutions the faculty members reported no use of these publications and the library does not systematically collect them. At the other private baccalaureate institutions only three faculty members use municipal publications.

The libraries of approximately 50 percent (97) of the social scientists using foreign documents do not systematically gather such publications. Over two-thirds (67) of these users are affiliated with private graduate institutions, but none of the libraries in this category collect foreign documents. The remaining social science users cluster at private baccalaureate (9) and public master's-level (18) institutions. As for public baccalaureate institutions, one accounted for three users and the other, which did not report having any users does not systematically gather foreign documents.

At least some of the social scientists from all the institutions use documents of the United Nations and of other international organizations, only eleven libraries collect these publications. The exceptions, all private institutions with degree programs below the doctorate, account for one-fifth (53 faculty members) of the use of the publications of this level of government. At one private baccalaureate institution, three social scientists consult publications from this government level, while the number of users at the rest of the noncollecting institutions ranges from six to eighteen.

Termination of the analysis at this point might be misleading as the libraries may supplement their holdings of government publications by participation in cooperative depositories or consortia. Therefore, use of the publications of a particular level of government was compared to whether or not the libraries belong to such arrangements.

As the library at the University of Notre Dame has membership in the Center for Research Libraries, faculty members presumably can borrow needed state publications from CRL through the university library. If the number of these individuals were deducted from the list of forty-four social scientists whose libraries do not systematically collect state publications, the adjusted number became twenty-nine. Therefore, only 12.7 percent of the faculty members using state publications cannot draw upon the resources of their institutions' libraries for such materials. Again, these libraries are all associated with private institutions with degree programs ranging from the baccalaureate to the doctorate.

In addition to the University of Notre Dame, two libraries, both parts of public graduate institutions, participate in cooperative arrangements through which municipal publications can be borrowed. The number of users from these institutions (twenty-six) was deducted from fifty-four, the total number of faculty members associated with noncollecting libraries. It was then found that over one-third of the social scientists utilizing municipal publications have institutional libraries not involved in pertinent collection-building activities. These institutions range from those offering the baccalaureate to those offering the doctorate.

Two private doctorate-granting institutions collecting foreign documents participate in cooperative arrangements, and they account for forty-eight users. This figure was deducted from ninety-seven, the faculty total for noncollecting institutions. Therefore, one-fifth of the faculty members utilizing foreign publications cannot rely upon the systematic collection-building of their institutional libraries. Thirty of these social scientists teach at master's-level institutions whereas twelve are associated with baccalaureate institutions and seven with doctoral institutions.

As for the social scientists using documents of the United Nations and other international organizations, all are associated with institutions in which the library either gathers such publications or has access to them through cooperative arrangements.

Ten of the social scientists interviewed (14.7 percent) draw upon publications from levels of government not collected by their library. Even those at research institutions appear to accept the fact that their libraries cannot collect all the source material that might be needed. To supplement their libraries' collections, they visit other libraries in the vicinity, including the University of Chicago, University of Illinois at Urbana, and Indiana University, Bloomington. In some cases, they wait until they are in Washington, D.C., and then use the resources of the Library of Congress and/or the National Archives.

One of the social scientists interviewed had received government publications which his library borrowed from the Center for Research Libraries (CRL). He found the service "very satisfactory." Five of the other faculty members whose libraries do not collect from specified levels of government explained that they had not previously thought about borrowing government publications on interlibrary loan. Apparently, libraries need to explain their ability to supplement selective depository holdings by drawing upon the resources of nearby regional depositories.

Of the seven faculty members who had used interlibrary loan facilities, only two did not find the process wholly satisfactory. For one it was too slow and the publications could not be held long enough. It was easier for him to drive to a nearby depository library which has a collection larger than his own institutional library and to borrow publications there for a longer time period than is permitted by interlibrary loan.

The other social scientist noted that it can be difficult to supply the complete information requested on interlibrary loan forms. Published sources might indicate that a census of France for 1860 to 1880 is available in twelve volumes, but they do not specify the contents of each volume. If she needs "occupational statistics," there may be no alternative but to drive to the University of Chicago, determine the correct volume, and then submit the request through the interlibrary loan department of her institutional library.

The seven social scientists who had used interlibrary loan felt that the process is a potential resource for their students. However, most of their students' needs can be met from the existing collections of their own depository libraries.

In summary, the hypothesis cannot be entirely accepted. The academic libraries under study do not all collect from, or have access to, the publications of the different levels of government needed and used by their clientele; this finding does not necessarily signify that all academic libraries should systematically collect from all of the levels of government. It was beyond the scope of the investigation to look at factors such as institutional mission statements, the number of faculty requests for sources held by consortia, proximity of supplementary collections, frequency of use of publications, and budget allocations. Still, the author must note that the number of faculty members using documents, but not being able to tap their own institutional libraries for needed publications, was significant. For example, at two graduate institutions fourteen faculty members use municipal publications and eighteen faculty members consult the publications of foreign governments. However, these libraries, for whatever reasons, do not systematically collect publications of these levels of government.

> H2   There is a statistically significant relationship between the frequency of faculty use of government publictions and:
>
>   (a)   the organization of the government publications collection (government publictions in integrated or mixed collections are used more heavily than documents kept in separate collections).

The chi square test disclosed no statistically significant difference between the frequency of documents use and the arrangement of the Federal publications collection (χ^2 (3,2) = 3.28, $p <$ .05). As shown in Table 5.3, social scientists, regardless of their frequency of documents use, rely as much upon the library's publications located entirely in separate collections as they do upon those found in mixed collections.

A comparison of frequency of documents use and the arrangement of the state publications (χ^2 (3,3) = 2.28, $p <$ .05) and municipal publications (χ^2 (3,2) = 1.57, $p <$ .05) collections did not produce statistically significant differences. Perhaps social scientists adjust their search strategies to accommodate local library circumstances. Before concluding the analysis, it might be noted that a brief discussion of frequency of documents use cannot detail search strategies and the importance and types of materials uncovered through each collection arrangement.

>   (b)   the classification scheme (use is greater when documents are classified according to widely known schemes such as the Library of Congress or Dewey than when specialized ones such as SUDOC are employed).

Chi square analysis for the data depicted in Table 5-4 indicated that there is no statistically significant difference between frequency of use and the type of classification scheme employed (χ^2 (3,2) = 6.93, $p <$ .05). Regardless of the

Table 5-3   Comparison of Collection Arrangement and Frequency of Documents Use

| Frequency of Documents Use | Collection Arrangements | | |
	Separate No. (%)	Incorporated into General Collection No. (%)	Mixed No. (%)
Heavy	87(37.5)	8(3.4)	137(59.1)
Moderate	64(41.8)	7(4.6)	82(53.6)
Limited	70(37.6)	4(2.2)	112(60.2)
Non-users	47(42.0)	3(2.7)	62(55.4)

frequency of documents use, social scientists are as likely to use Federal publications housed solely under a separate collection employing a specialized scheme as they are to use publications found in another type of collection arrangement employing a more widely known classification scheme. Examination of the classification schemes used for publications of state (χ^2 (3,3) = 2.48, $p < .05$) and municipal (χ^2 (3,3) = 1.03, $p < .05$) governments disclosed the identical pattern as that for Federal government publications.

(c)   the percentage of depository items received

As shown in Table 5-2, the only percentage categories not represented in this study are those for regional depositories and for the receipt of less than 10 percent of the depository items. According to a recent survey, approximately 11 percent of the depository libraries take less than 10 percent of the SUDOC depository categories. However, only fifty-six of these libraries are associated with academic institutions (Whitbeck, Hernon, & Richardson, 1978, 253-267). Because of this small number, the libraries under study seem to provide a cross-section of the larger, medium-sized, and smaller depository collections.

Chi square analysis did not disclose any statistically significant differences between frequency of documents use and the percentage of depository items received (χ^2 (3,5) = 13.12, $p < .05$). Approximately two-thirds to three-fourths of the heavy, moderate, and limited users are associated with institutional libraries receiving more than 69 percent of the categories. However, as these institutions have larger faculties, the study does not show that use is a function of collection size.

(d)   the percentage of government publications entered into the public card catalog

An assumption might be that the heavier documents users are associated with institutions in which the libraries enter a larger percentage of government publications into the card catalog. However, as Table 5-5 depicts, documents users cluster at institutions in which the libraries catalog less than 30 percent of

Table 5-4   Comparisons of Classification Scheme
to Frequency of Documents Use

| Frequency of Documents Use | Classification Schemes | | |
	SUDOC No. (%)	LC No. (%)	Mixed No. (%)
Heavy	104(44.8)	8(3.4)	120(51.7)
Moderate	68(44.4)	7(4.6)	78(51.0)
Limited	77(41.4)	4(2.2)	105(56.5)
Non-users	61(54.5)	3(2.7)	48(42.9)

Table 5-5 Comparison of Percentage of Federal
Publications Cataloged to Frequency
of Documents Use

Frequency of Documents Use	Percentage of Publications Cataloged					
	Over 90 No. (%)	49-30 No. (%)	29-10 No. (%)	Under 10 No. (%)	Unspecified No. (%)	Total
Heavy	8(3.4)	22(9.5)	76(32.8)	103(44.4)	23(9.9)	232(100)
Moderate	7(4.6)	11(7.2)	47(30.7)	73(47.7)	15(9.8)	153(100)
Limited	4(2.2)	18(9.7)	58(31.2)	87(46.7)	19(10.2)	186(100)

the Federal publications. Of course, only one of the libraries prepared catalog cards for over 50 percent of its United States publications.

Less than half the libraries collecting state publications enter catalog cards for them in the public card catalog. Those which most often catalog them do so for less than 10 percent of the items. The chi square test examining frequency of documents use reflects this distribution (χ^2 (3,2) = 6.28, $p < .05$). A similar pattern emerges for a comparison of frequency of documents use to the inclusion of municipal publications in the public card catalog (χ^2 (3,2) = 6.2, $p < .05$).

Over one-half (153, or 63.8 percent) of the 240 social scientists consulting the card catalog do not use state government publications. Of those who do, nine (3.7 percent) are at institutions where the libraries catalog over 90 percent, and the remaining seventy-eight faculty members (32.5 percent) are associated with institutions where the libraries enter less than 10 percent of the government publications into the public catalog.

Only 20 percent of the social scientists using the card catalogs desire municipal publications. Five of them, or 10.4 percent, are associated with institutional libraries cataloging over 90 percent and the remaining forty-three, or 89.6 percent, are affiliated with libraries cataloging less than 10 percent of the documents.

In summary, the card catalog is apparently used more extensively by social scientists seeking Federal government publications than by those searching for state and municipal government publications.

(e) the number of staff members employed in the servicing of government publications

The chi square test did not show a statistically significant relationship between frequency of documents use and the total number of documents staff (χ^2 (3,11) = 24.95, $p < .05$), number of professional staff (χ^2 (3,6) = 11.95, $p < .05$), number of clerical personnel (χ^2 (3,3) = 4.88, $p < .05$), and number of paraprofessional employees (χ^2 (3,5) = 5.48, $p < .05$). As a result, the assumption that use is influenced by a large number of staff is unsubstantiated by the findings of the study.

The size of staff is relatively homogeneous across institutions. It may be that staffing merits further investigation, perhaps with an examination of such variables as internal library organization, division of responsibilities, number of hours the library and the documents department are open per week, and time periods in which service is provided.

(f)   the circulation of government publications to faculty members

This hypothesis could not be examined fully due to the skewing of the findings in favor of those libraries circulating government publications. Only two libraries (11.8 percent) do not circulate documents, and they are situated in private graduate institutions. A total of 67.9 percent of the documents users, regardless of their frequency of use, are associated with institutions in which libraries circulate these publications. Therefore, the chi square test did not disclose a statistically significant difference between whether or not documents circulate and frequency of use (χ^2 (3,1) = .89, $p < .05$). However, as has already been noted, the topic of circulation merits further investigation.

(g)   1.   whether or not the library has a regular program for informing faculty and students of important government publications (those libraries promoting use have the greatest level of documents use).

2.   faculty members' awareness of the variety of programs offered.

Fourteen, or 82.4 percent, of the libraries reported having regular programs for publicizing government publications, whereas only three, or 17.7 percent, of them do *not* have such "outreach" programs; these three are all associated with private institutions offering graduate programs. The chi square test indicated that the first hypothesis cannot be accepted since the difference was not statistically significant (χ^2 (2,3) = 3.52, $p < .05$). Approximately 15 percent of the documents users, regardless of frequency of use, are associated with institutions in which the libraries do not have such programs.

The librarians in charge of the government publications collections were asked to specify the method(s) employed by their libraries to enhance faculty and student awareness of important government publications. As depicted in Table 5-6, the librarians rely most frequently on a relatively few methods: displays, tours, and library lectures provided to classroom instruction; other methods were listed by less than one-third of the libraries having regular programs. It might be noted, however, that five of the libraries offer courses on library usage, either credit or noncredit, in which government publications are introduced.

The librarians were not asked to provide data on the frequency with which they resort to particular means for promoting documents utilization nor to

Table 5-6   Promotional Devices Employed by Librarians
Offering a Regular Outreach Program

Number	Promotional Techniques
11	Setting up displays
11	Tours (orientation and instructional)
8	Library lectures conducted through the classroom
6	Maintaining documents bulletin boards
5	Preparation of bibliographic guides to specific disciplines

evaluate the effectiveness of one means in relationship to another. One library did supply its *Annual Report 1976-77,* in which it was mentioned that ninety-six different classes received instruction in the use of indexes to government publications and an awareness of those publications pertinent to specific class needs. One librarian reported that "insufficient library staff and budgetary restrictions make it impossible to implement as many methods as we feel would be of benefit to our students and faculty."

The replies to the library questionnaire item seeking the methods used for publicizing documents corresponded to those presented on the faculty questionnaire. Because of this, an attempt was made to compare faculty perceptions against the actual list of programs. As was mentioned in Chapter 4, 302, or 44.2 percent, of the social scientists believe that their libraries have no regular programs, or they admit that they have no idea of the method(s) used. It would seem that many faculty members, regardless of their frequency of documents use, are guessing; some of them even admitted that this is the case.

It might be hypothesized that faculty members benefitting from a particular method are the ones most likely to be aware of that method. As support for this contention, it was found that 80 percent of the faculty members whose students receive classroom instruction are the ones who have invited a librarian to provide specialized instruction in the use of the library.

> H3   Faculty members associated with institutions whose libraries incorporate government publications into the general collection are not more likely to browse for documents than are their counterparts at institutions in which the libraries' documents collections are separate.

As was explained in Chapter 4, 177 social scientists acknowledged browsing as a means for locating needed Federal government publications. Seventy-one, or 40.1 percent, of them are at institutions where libraries arrange all their government publications in separate collections, predominantly by the Superintendent of Documents Classification System (SUDOC), whereas ninety-nine, or 55.9 percent, of the faculty members are associated with institutional libraries having mixed documents collections. The remaining seven of them, or 4 percent, use integrated collections. Therefore, hypothesis H3 cannot be fully studied due to the skewing of data by the number of faculty members associated with institutions whose libraries either totally separate or mix their collections of government publications.

Sixty-two of the faculty members who engage in browsing (35 percent) do not use state publications. Of those remaining, seventy-nine, or 44.6 percent, have access to mixed collections; and thirty-four, or 19.2 percent, consult entirely separate collections; two, or 1 percent, use integrated collections. Over one-fourth of the faculty browsers (fifty, or 28.2 percent) use municipal publications, and predominantly they have access to mixed collections (thirty, or 60 percent).

SUMMARY

The first part of this chapter provides a descriptive overview of basic characteristics for the libraries associated with the seventeen institutions under study. The second part examines hypotheses based on certain characteristics of the collection of government publications held by the libraries.

These hypotheses have been based on assumptions long and widely held by documents librarians. The assumptions relate to the belief that library clientele would probably use documents more if they were filed with other materials on the same subject and were arranged by a widely known subject classification scheme (Ruth M. Erlander in Boyd & Rips, 1949, p. 591). As one librarian hypothesized:

> Users expect the catalog to record all books in the library, whether those books happen to be published by the government or by the book trade. If the holdings of the library are not card-indexed, patrons will be hindered in their work. There are many who do not realize the existence of government publications, who do not think to ask the one in charge if there is additional material not listed in the catalog (Ruth M. Erlander in Boyd & Rips, 1949, p. 575).

It might have been assumed in this study that there would be a statistically significant difference between frequency of documents use and such variables as the organization of the collection, the classification scheme, the percentage of depository items received, the percentage of government publications entered in the public catalog, the number of staff members servicing government publications, and whether or not the library circulated government publications. However, these variables did not emerge as statistically significant.

The hypotheses are exploratory in nature and make a beginning in an area in need of research. Given their general nature, the hypotheses cannot detail the impact of the variables described on the frequency of documents use, on the process by which faculty members locate needed materials held by the library, or on the importance, if any, to which they attach publications listed in the public catalog.

6. Comparison of Findings to Previous Research

This chapter relates the findings of this investigation to those of previous studies of documents use (Danielson, 1973, 139-146; Hernon & Williams, 1976, 93-108; McCaghy & Purcell, 1972, 7-12; McIlvaine, 1975, 49-51; Wilson, 1973, 76-80). Comparisons, however, are imprecise due to different populations surveyed, dissimilar questionnaire emphasis and phraseology, and variations in return rates and the type of data reported. Also, only one of the use studies covered in Chapter 2 analyzed data by specific disciplines within the social sciences.

The studies depicted in Table 6-1 have not all employed identical categories to define frequency of documents use. For example, the time intervals of the categories, such as "1 to 2 times a semester" and "1 to 2 times a year," are different. Also, previous studies did not relate use to a reference time frame such as a particular academic year. Because of these limitations, the present study used different categories based upon an estimation of use for a specific time period. For the purpose of a crude comparison, however, it is assumed here that there may be similarities between heavy use and "2 or 3 times a month," moderate use and "1 or 2 times a semester," and limited use and "1 or 2 times a year."

A total of fifty-five social scientists responded to the University of Connecticut study and twenty-five, or 45.5 percent, of them were infrequent users (used documents once a semester or less). Some forty-eight respondents to the Trinity University study were social scientists, and twenty, or 35 percent, of the faculty members who rarely or never used the documents collection were in the social sciences. For the University of Nebraska at Omaha study, some 130 of the respondents were social scientists. A total of 19 percent of them "never" used government publications and 25 percent consulted them "1 to 2 times a year." The Case Western Reserve University study reported that 55 percent of the respondents were social scientists but did not separate their use from that of the humanities faculty members.

As shown in Table 6-1, the Case Western Reserve survey found that 62 percent of the faculty members do not use the documents collection. However, this percentage included those who consult government publications held by other libraries and who obtain personal copies. If these individuals are deducted from the total, the percentage of faculty members who never use government publications is reduced to 35. The other three use studies did not report data in such a way that non-users of the government publications collection could be separated from non-users of government publications.

In the present study, only 16.4 percent of the respondents do not use the documents collection. By deducting those who are not members of the faculty the previous year, who consult the government publications' holdings of other libraries, and who obtain personal copies, the percentage is reduced to 13.9. Comparison of this percentage to those of the other studies shows a large difference, which *may* be accounted for by the fact that this study concentrated entirely on the social sciences and did not include disciplines in which the need for government publications might be marginal.

Past surveys found that the major reason for non-use of government publications was that faculty members felt that they were not required for their work. The University of Nebraska at Omaha survey used the same categorization as did the other studies, but it disclosed that during the interview phase some faculty members who marked this response were actually unaware of the existence of government publications relevant to their professional needs. Because of this finding, the present study modified the category to reflect the perception that "government publishes little or nothing of value in my immediate field." Limited users and non-users cite this as the major reason for their infrequent use of government publications.

A comparison of general library use to use of the documents collection showed variation among the use studies. The data for the Case Western Reserve survey are skewed by the large percentage of faculty members who do not use the documents collection. The authors conclude that there is a weak relationship. Analysis of the data of the Trinity University survey suggests that responses were evenly distributed among the categories for frequency of documents use and that four-fifths of the respondents (80 percent) are frequent library users. Only three faculty members use the library either infrequently or never. Twenty-nine percent of the frequent users of the library are also frequent users of the documents collection, and approximately the same percentage of frequent

Table 6-1 Frequency of Use for Government Publications Held by College or University Library

Frequency	Case Western Reserve University (McCaghy and Purcell)[2] (n = 103) %	Trinity University (Wilson) (n = 100) %	University of Connecticut[1] (McIlvanine) (n = 108) %	University of Nebraska at Omaha (Hernon and Williams) (N = 218) %	Multicampus study (n = 683) %
2-3 times a month	1	23	16	18	34.0
1-2 times a semester	14	19	19	26	22.4
1-2 times a year	23	26	31	25	27.2
Never	62	32	34	31	16.4

[1] The Connecticut study modified the categories for frequency of use as follows: several times a month, once a month, once a semester, and less frequently.
[2] Number of respondents.

library users never consult the documents collection (28). A similar pattern emerged with the University of Connecticut study, where responses were also evenly distributed among the categories for frequency of documents use and where over half of the respondents are frequent users of the library.

For the present study the data are skewed by the large number of faculty members whose library use is heavy. These social scientists account for 67.2 percent (454) of the use of the documents collections. Chi square analysis, as was shown in Chapter 4, indicates a strong relationship between frequency of library use and of documents use. However, as in the studies of Trinity University and the University of Connecticut, responses were evenly distributed among the categories provided for frequency of documents use.

Past use studies have not all reported comparable information on the frequency by which faculty members request assistance from library staff members. It appears that the percentage of faculty members never requesting assistance varies, but the maximum percentage reported was 23. For the present investigation, the percentage of those never requesting assistance is comparable: 20 percent. Comparison of the other categories for the questionnaire item is complicated by the different terminology employed. If the category of "more than 50 percent of the time" is equated to the combined categories of "frequently" and "always," the percentage reported by the study of Case Western Reserve University is 28; Trinity University, 15; and University of Nebraska at Omaha, 26. The percentage for the present study is 27.4.

The Case Western Reserve University study found that most of the users of the documents collection express satisfaction with the assistance given by the library staff members. Similarly the present investigation discloses a small percentage (7.2) of faculty members reluctant to request assistance in using the collection.

Previous research has tried to determine the ways in which faculty members who generally do not require assistance in using the collection locate needed government publications. Comparison here is impaired by the fact that category options varied considerably reflecting local circumstances. It suffices to say that faculty members seem to find information on government publications through citations in the literature or special bibliographies of their subject field, browsing in the collection, and consulting appropriate indexes. The present investigation also found that social scientists rely on their subject literature and indexes. Browsing, on the other hand, receives less emphasis. Regardless of the discipline, faculty members listed it as the fifth choice. Greater reliance is placed on sources already familiar to them and on the public card catalog. Social scientists also make considerable use of mailing lists, personal contacts, and citations from colleagues as means for locating needed government publications.

Past studies have emphasized that faculty members have only limited knowledge of the bibliographic tools that provide access to government publications. Awareness of indexes often does not extend beyond the *Monthly Catalog of United States Government Publications,* the now defunct *Price Lists,* and perhaps ERIC *Resources in Education.* Table 4-10 displays the guides and indexes used by those faculty members associated with the present investigation. Approximately one-fourth of the documents users do not consult any index. Those who do use the indexes often consult relatively few titles. The five most frequently mentioned indexes, and percentages of social scientists consulting them, are as follows: *Index to U.S. Government Periodicals* (47.4), *Monthly Catalog* (43.8), *Selected U.S. Government Publications* (30.4), retrospective indexes (30.2), and *CIS Index* (19.5). As was shown in Chapter 4, many interview subjects have limited awareness of indexes, even of those that might be potentially beneficial. However, they indicate that awareness does not necessarily signify use. They state that they are often able to find the information desired by bypassing the indexes and consulting library staff members or browsing.

The Case Western Reserve University study, in an effort to determine if the age pattern matched the publishing history of the *Monthly Catalog,* ascertained the age of the government publications most often consulted. Sixty-five percent of those faculty members answering the question relating to the age of needed publications seek sources issued within the previous five years, while 75 percent of them need materials less than ten years of age. Because of this finding, it was concluded that "a basic knowledge of how the *Monthly Catalog* works should enable these users to find the items they want" (McCaghy & Purcell, 1972, 11).

The authors of the University of Nebraska at Omaha study reached a similar conclusion. They found that, except for historians, social scientists generally prefer government publications not over five years old; in many cases, the more current the better. The authors concluded that social scientists, since they lack familiarity with specific indexes, are "not getting access to all available resources" (Hernon & Williams, 1976, 98).

The present study found that social scientists (other than historians) rely upon government publications of a current nature, generally less than three years of age. However, a statement about the age of the material sought has not been used to suggest that a knowledge of indexes may be beneficial. Faculty members may only want awareness of publications held by their particular library. Also, comparisons of ages and indexes would have to take into consideration such factors as index comprehensiveness and the time lag between the date of publication for a document and its appearance in a published index or on the shelf of a library. For example, a recent study found that the time lag from the date a document was received by the library and the date that the *Montly Catalog* listed it was 168 ± 8 days (95 percent confidence) (Boast & Nyberg, 1978, 172). Another study has discovered that 79.7 percent of the Congressional publications listed in the *CIS Index* appear in the *Monthly Catalog* and that on an average, these publications are available over one hundred days earlier in the *CIS Index* (Harrison, 1978, 273-283).

The University of Nebraska at Omaha study disclosed that the majority of faculty respondents learn to locate government publications by a process of trial-and-error, sometimes combined with informal instruction from a librarian. The means of learning to locate publications has little relationship to the frequency of documents use, since the percentage of those who learn by the process of trial-and-error and who also use documents frequently (34 percent) is nearly the same as those who learn through a formal course (37 percent) or through informal instruction by librarians (35 percent). The group in which the largest proportion use government publications frequently is the one in which faculty members learn through process of self-instruction.

One of the hypotheses in Chapter 4 (H11) states that "there is no statistically significant difference among faculty members as to how they learned to find materials in the documents collection." On the basis of the data presented, the null hypothesis was accepted. The major means by which they learn to find the materials is by trial-and-error in actually using the collection, informal instruction from the library staff, and self-instruction. Considerably fewer of the responding social scientists have taken formal courses involving documents utilization (29).

Only the survey at Northwestern University reported percentages of faculty use across the publications of different levels of government. It found that the publications of the United States government receive the most extensive use (57 percent), followed by those of the United Nations (16 percent), other international organizations (9 percent), state and local governments (9 percent), and foreign governments (8 percent). However, these percentages are based upon the responses of only seventeen faculty members.

The present investigation found similarities as to the levels of government of which publications are consulted. Regardless of discipline, the publications of the Federal government are used by the largest number of social scientists, those of the United Nations and other international agencies by the next largest number; those of state governments place third. The publications of foreign and municipal governments receive considerably less use.

The study at the University of Nebraska at Omaha found that 42 percent of the faculty members, both document users and non-users, do not alert their students to the value of government publications. Some 41 percent of the documents users do not attempt to make students aware of these publications. The remaining 59 percent rely mostly on an informal method, that of "suggesting the collection as a valuable source of information." For the present investigation, approximately one-fourth of the social scientists, comprising both users and non-users, do not make students aware of the documents collection. As shown in Chapter 4 for H22, there is a difference (not statistically tested) between heavy and moderate users, and limited users and non-users. Still, the most frequently marked categories were those "suggesting the collection as a valuable source of information" and for "referring students to a library."

On the basis of questionnaire and interview findings, the present investigation found that certain assumptions and conclusions of previous studies are not applicable to the sample surveyed. The author of the University of Connecticut survey suggested that documents use can be increased by the inclusion of more entries for documents in the card catalog (McIlvaine, 1975, 49), and the author of the Northwestern University study concluded that ". . . users need to be reminded that government publications are not usually listed in the main card catalog" (Danielson, 1973, 145). The present study disclosed that only two of the libraries studied do not enter government publications in the public card catalog and that only one of the libraries cataloging documents does so for more than 50 percent of its collection. As shown in H10 of Chapter 4, social scientists as a group list the card catalog as the fourth most important means for locating documents. Examination of respondents by discipline indicates that the card catalog is mentioned fourth by economists, historians, and political scientists, but second by sociologists.

Interview subjects were also asked how they locate needed government publications held by the library. For these faculty members, the card catalog is seldom regarded as a major resource in their search for source material. They realize that documents are selectively cataloged. For some of them, consulting the card catalog comprises an added step to the literature search process, one which is not likely to be productive. It is a "time-saver" to bypass the card catalog and to consult indexes, browse, or ask library staff members for assistance.

The findings of the present investigation are reinforced by those of the study conducted at Case Western Reserve University, where it was found that only nine, or 39 percent, of the faculty members use the public card catalog to locate documents and that the major approach to documents is through the subject literature. Therefore, the authors concluded that if most of the users do not consult the card catalog, depository libraries maintaining separate documents collections need to rethink the necessity of cataloging government publications (McCaghy & Purcell, 1972, 12).

Another assumption of two of the earlier studies was that if faculty members were made aware of government publications pertinent to their teaching and research interests, they would use these publications (Hernon & Williams, 1976, 96; McIlvaine, 1975, 49). During the interviews for the present investigation, however, it was found that this assumption may be invalid. A number of factors may enter the picture and prevent social scientists from following through on leads. For example, they may more readily find comparable data for teaching through other sources such as newspapers.

Previous documents use studies conducted within the United States have focused upon faculty members associated with a particular institution. The most comprehensive survey of social scientists, however, was conducted in the United Kingdom. Between September 1967 and December 1970, a national investigation into the information requirements of the social sciences was conducted at the University of Newcastle upon Tyne and later at the University of Bath (*Invesitgation into Information Requirements of the Social Sciences,* 1971). For purposes of the investigation the social sciences were defined as the disciplines of anthropology, economics, education, political science, psychology, and sociology. Formal departments of history were excluded. The only historians represented in the survey were those associated with departments such as economics.

In the English study a mail questionnaire (pretested) and selected interviews were used to ascertain the information needs of social science researchers and educators associated with institutions of higher education, government departments, research institutions, and industry. Some 1,089 completed questionnaires were returned, and these represented a response rate of 41.8 percent.

Because of the different populations surveyed and the difference in questionnaire emphasis, comparisons between the British study and the present investigation must be imprecise and general. The British study did include "government publications and other official documents (e.g., U.N.)" as one of the physical forms for information but did not differentiate among levels of govenrnment publishing it.

In their comparison of disciplines and physical forms for information, the project staff members found that:

> Economists stood apart from other users, as they did not use monographs and theses as frequently as others, but were much more likely to use government publications. Political scientists were also heavy users of government publications, although not as heavy as economists. (*Investigation into Information Requirements of the Social Sciences,* 1971, 55)

Sociologists, to a lesser degree, find government publications an important information resource, whereas historians seldom utilize these publications. As was shown in discussing hypothesis three of Chapter 2, economists and political scientists are also the heaviest users of government publications. Historians situated in the four midwestern states make greater use of government publications than do those historians who participated in the British study. However, it should be repeated that the discipline of history is better represented in the present investigation.

The British study found that social scientists make fairly frequent use of government publications and that only 23 percent of the respondents never use this type of source material. For the present study the percentage is comparable (13.9).

One of the questionnaire items for the British survey asked social scientists about the kinds of information they need for current research. They were given six categories from which to choose; these were not intended to be mutually exclusive. The project staff members found that documents are heavily used to locate statistical and descriptive information.[1] (*Investigation into Information Requirements of the Social Sciences*, 1971, 59)

The present investigation did not use similar categories. As was shown in hypothesis 6 of Chapter 4, faculty members within any one of the disciplines do not differ significantly from those in any of the other disciplines as to the purpose(s) for which they consult government publications. The relationships between disciplines range from moderate to strong. Economists and sociologists consult government publications for census or normative data, while historians seek information of historical value. Political scientists mainly want census or normative data or a means of keeping abreast of current events and issues of interest.

Respondents to the British study were asked about the necessity for knowing of new sources very soon after publication. Some 84 percent of them felt that it was very or moderately important (*Investigation into Information Requirements of the Social Sciences*, 1971, 114). For the present study, the emphasis was also on current information. Those social scientists interviewed who rely on recent information stressed that they need to be aware of, and to gain access to, publications soon after they become available.

The project staff members for the British study also noted that:

> Even in the areas of primary interest, clients often stated that the problem was not so much one of knowledge of what has been and is being published in a given area, but rather that the vast amount of material, even in fairly specialized fields, makes selectivity and evaluation a necessity. (*Investigation into Information Requirements of the Social Sciences*, 1971, 127)

Interview subjects for the present investigation did not all hold a similar opinion. They commented on the number and variety of publications produced by governments. Some of them try to keep abreast of the proliferation of source material, whereas others find the extent of government publishing overwhelming and want to monitor the publications most important to their professional needs.

Citation studies provide another means for confirming findings on the use of government publications in social science literature. However, such studies have not been reported for all of the disciplines under investigation. Also, the reported studies do not all analyze the same types of literature.[2] Still, analysis of seven studies reported by one author suggest that government publications comprise an important information resource, especially for economists (Weech, 1978, 177-184).

[1]The category of descriptive information was not defined but was presented with the examples of marriage ceremonies of an African tribe and social life in a mining village.

[2] "Some of the studies drew their citations from books on the subject, while others used subject journals as their population for analysis. Those drawing data from books . . . found a higher percentage of citations to government publications than did studies of the same subject areas drawing data from journals. Whether this reflects a difference in type of research or in citation behavior of the authors of books as opposed to authors of journal articles, or if it is due to other factors, cannot be determined from the studies listed." (Weech, 1978, 179)

7. Increasing Documents Utilization

As shown in previous chapters, social scientists do use government publications, but they most frequently use those obtained from information-based institutions or agents other than libraries. Library use of this genre by social scientists is often limited to a few types of publications. The purpose of this chapter is to suggest ways to increase the utilization of the resources contained in depository library collections.

INTEGRATION OF DOCUMENTS IN GENERAL REFERENCE TOOLS

Some general reference collections include the *Monthly Catalog of United States Government Publications* but few of the other indexes which supplement this more general index. Consequently, there has been some discussion in library literature as to the most strategic location for specialized government indexes if there is a separate documents unit in the library. Some documents librarians advocate their retention in general reference collections, whereas others favor their location in separate collections. Each method has certain advantages; however, documents librarians encounter logistic problems when they must maneuver between separate collections and general reference collections located on different floors. Moreover, it is too expensive for most libraries to purchase duplicate copies of major indexes and to place them in various strategic locations. The result is that many people benefiting from government information may not find their way to separate documents collections. Still, those who consult documents collections undoubtedly receive more complete service, due in part to ready access to the more specialized reference tools.

Undoubtedly, many library users are unaware that documents might be appropriate to their information needs. The problem may be due, in part, to the fact that documents are not widely included in existing general reference tools. For example, periodicals issued by the Government Printing Office are only selectively covered in traditional indexes. *PAIS Bulletin* provides more extended coverage of government periodicals[1] than *Readers Guide, Social Science Index, Business Periodical Index, Social Science Citation Index,* and other general indexes which analyse significantly fewer of these periodicals. In 1976 *Readers Guide,* for example, indexed only four of the more general government periodicals (McClure, 1978, 421). Evidently government periodicals are not widely recognized by general index producers as a major information source. Because of this lack, a specialized *Index to U.S. Government Periodicals* is available and perhaps should be housed in general reference collections. Support for this recommendation is seen from the fact that survey subjects cited this index more frequently than they did any other government-related index (see H17 of Chapter 4).

PUBLIC CARD CATALOGS

It is too expensive for most libraries with large and separate collections of government publications to rely on public card catalogs as the primary means for documents retrieval. These libraries should use signs and posters, specifying that documents holdings are only partially reflected in card catalogs, encouraging users to visit documents collections, and explaining the significance of depository status. It would be desirable if the Government Printing Office, which provides depository publications gratis on the stipulation that the

---

[1] A comparative analysis of periodical indexing indicated that *PAIS Bulletin* included thirty-seven periodicals in the 1976 edition. Yet, two of the more specialized government related indexes analyzed 156 and 894 periodicals respectively for the same time period (McClure, 5 (1978), 412).

The inclusion criteria for *PAIS Bulletin* state that "because of the immense output, it is not possible to index all United States government publications falling within the scope of PAIS. Priority in selection is governed generally by the importance of the document's subject matter as an issue of national policy and the amount of new information it contains." *PAIS Bulletin* includes a cross section of different types of government publications. "Congressional hearings and committee prints, and reports and studies of other federal agencies, are included as fully as space permits;" ". . . special compilations of laws pertaining to a single subject are generally included." Other types of documents are included only if they have "unusual policy relevance" ("PAIS Selection Policy," *PAIS Bulletin,* 63 (1977), ix).

materials be accessible to the public, could develop a budgetary category for funding research on depository libraries and for alerting the public to the existence of depository collections at nearby libraries.

During the interview phase of this investigation, social scientists volunteered that their library was a depository for Federal publications. However, they were often unsure what this entailed or perhaps presented misinformation. Perhaps the Government Printing Office should develop short, explanatory handouts for distribution to library clientele.

Libraries selecting only a small percentage of documents categories could maintain collections, with holdings accessible through the main public card catalog. These libraries could obtain catalog cards such as those produced through the OCLC system. However, since many social scientists and perhaps other user groups bypass card catalogs in their search for government publications, signs and other publicity measures would have to inform them that card catalogs do reflect documents holdings.

Typically, government publications are selectively cataloged and entered into the main public card catalog. Conceivably, some users who have found citations to documents in traditional indexes do consult card catalogs but do not find reference to the desired publication(s). If they do not realize that documents are retained in separate collections, they may terminate their search for the item(s) at this point or may seek alternative information sources. Even when card catalogs indicate that a particular publication is located in a special collection, can it be assumed that users can correctly interpret codes and locate desired sources? Moreover, the question may well be posed as to what extent librarians, particularly those in public service positions, function as gate-keepers in discouraging use of documents by the public, whether through ignorance of governmental structure or publishing, of bibliographic tools, or of accessing methods. It is hypothesized that librarians unfamiliar with government publications may shy away from referring users to these sources and from helping to exploit documents.

Research has shown that "most people do not persevere very long in catalog searches. More than 50% will look up only one entry and then stop, regardless of whether or not they have found what they are looking for. Most subject searches are attempted under a single subject heading" (Lancaster, 1977, p. 70). One study found that library users at one academic institution frequently access Federal publications through subject entries in the card catalog (DeVelbiss, 1956). It might be questioned if documents need to be entered by corporate author, title, and by subject. Many users experience difficulty negotiating massive numbers of cards under "U.S." and its various subdivisions. It would be desirable to explore the possibility of computer retrieval of materials, organized so that there is no distinction by publisher of information or by levels of government.

DOCUMENTS "OUTREACH" PROGRAMS

Given the fact that many depository library collections are operated by a small number of staff, preoccupied with collection development and maintenance, it is understandable that documents "outreach" programs are not well developed (Whitbeck, Hernon, & Richardson, 1978, 253-267). Still, depository libraries should experiment with different activities, some of which could be quickly and easily accomplished whereas others admittedly would be time-consuming and produce mixed results.

"Outreach" activities fall under three goals: (1) increasing user awareness, (2) acquainting or orienting users with library facilities, and (3) instructing clientele in the use of libraries, commonly referred to as "bibliographic instruction." The first goal encompasses alerting people to the fact that libraries are primary sources of information and a principal means for meeting information requirements. Through such activities non-users can become aware of library resources and realize that documents collections may contain information applicable to their needs. With the second goal, users are familiarized with library facilities and services, including physical layout, procedures, and staff. They become acquainted with the location of separate documents collections, documents staff members, the hours during which the documents reference service is provided, and circulation policies. The final goal, which is instructional, encompasses helping users to take maximum advantage of library resources in meeting their information requirements. As a result of instruction, there should be improvement in library skills and less dependence on library staff members for finding information contained in the collection.

In order to increase user awareness, librarians should portray their libraries as government depositories, explain the significance of depository status, and inform users about the types of information contained in the collection. To accomplish these tasks, librarians can select from among such approaches as the preparation of displays, bulletin boards, signs, brochures, short filmstrips, and videotapes; advertisements and articles for student and local newspapers; campus radio and television announcements; current awareness service; a section in library handbooks and guides on depository collections; and statements about the library as a depository for inclusion in college catalogs. In addition, librarians might find it useful to meet with faculty members individually or at departmental meetings, have a separate listing for depository collections in local telephone directories, and integrate documents into the central browsing corner or shelf of libraries.

In the literature of documents librarianship some writers have explained techniques for increasing user awareness of depository collections. In the opinion of one author, the first task is to alert library staff members to the significance of documents and then to extend the publicity campaign to other segments of the academic community (Murrell, 1950). In the early 1940s the

Florida State College for Women tried to make faculty members and students more aware of government publications. Those faculty members teaching in the disciplines of political science, economics, geography, social welfare, home economics, and social studies received letters notifying them that the library was a depository for publications of the Government Printing Office, alerting them to the value of these resources, and inviting utilization of the collection. Upon faculty request, librarians set up special exhibits of those documents relevant to a discipline in the reference room. Apparently "the response to the letter was immediate and enthusiastic. Classes came to the library to have the documents explained to them, and faculty came not only to study the documents but also to request special exhibits as suggested in the letter." The exhibits were also reported in the college newspaper. On the basis of the initial reception, other exhibits were planned (Haynes & Coykendall, 1943, 544). Exhibits may correct errorneous impressions that government publications constitute only archival-type records or small pamphlets or folders such as home and garden bulletins. Exhibits may also begin dialogue with users about the types of resources they need and the problems they encounter in accessing this information.

Displays can be most effective if they are strategically located in the library and throughout the campus. Those set up in separate documents departments have limited impact. They will be seen only by those who come to the department and already know or suspect that documents will meet some of their information requirements.

Documents librarians may find it useful to write occasional articles for local newspapers in which they highlight documents of high interest to the general public. They can circulate informational and recreational pamphlets to anyone expressing interest. Librarians might approach their Congressional representatives for multiple copies of particular pamphlets, so that requested items need not be returned. Such a service might encourage people to consider government publications as a potential information resource.

To address the orientation-related goal, librarians can develop handbooks, tours of the library and documents collection, and bibliographic guides for specific disciplines. The tours can be self-guided and dependent on such visual aids as directional signs and wall diagrams, with or without handbooks, to show the major features of the department.

Orientation tours can be offered to interested groups. For example, elementary school students touring libraries can be introduced to depository collections by having them examine census block maps in order to pinpoint where they live; they might also be shown maps and photographs taken from different probes of outer space.

Librarians should ascertain the specific research and teaching interests of new faculty members and invite them to a library orientation in which sources including government publications of potential interest to these areas are shown.

In individual discussions librarians can expand upon the list of potentially useful sources. As a result, faculty members will become acquainted with those librarians who can serve as liasons on library-related matters, become aware of the "outreach" programs which might be beneficial to their students, and have realistic expectations regarding the capabilities of their students in using the documents collection. They also become aware of the strengths and limitations of the documents collection and discover that through inter-library cooperation, the amount of source material at their disposal can be increased. At the same time, librarians gain a better understanding of user needs and discover some reason why instructors may *not* be drawing upon a wide range of specialized reference tools—it may be that libraries are retaining and acquiring reference tools whose cost is out of proportion to their benefit, present or potential.

An instructional role adds another dimension to documents reference service. Instruction in the use of documents collections and sources can be traced back to the early part of this century. However, many of the programs have been implemented on a limited scale, and little research has been conducted in this area. The research might be descriptive and reflect the current state-of-the-art, or experimental investigations evaluating different programs and approaches.

Bibliograhic instruction has been accomplished by class lectures, tours, term paper clinics and reference rap sessions (at prearranged times, students receive extensive assistance with class papers and projects), cassette taped instruction outlining the steps for conducting legislative histories, special seminars and workshops, formal courses on library usage, and computer-assisted instruction which might suggest how to search specific indexes or to negotiate separate documents collections arranged by specialized classification schemes.

Students constitute the primary target group for many of the instructional approaches. For example, instructional library lectures conducted through the classroom have been a popular method of library instruction as reflected in the literature of documents librarianship. These lectures are course related and generally chart library skills necessary to complete assignments. They are intended to familiarize students with library staff members, library policies and procedures, research literature, and search strategies. In some cases, after delivering the lecture, documents librarians leave the sources discussed on book charts in the documents department for students to peruse at their convenience.

As an alternative to formal lectures, a short presentation can be made and a list of the sources discussed distributed. The remaining part of the class period can then be devoted to examining indexes and catalogs for source material pertinent to class projects. After several citations have been located, students can be shown how to find documents arranged by the Superintendent of Documents Classification Scheme.

Faculty members may want to be informed of current library developments that can aid their library research, for example, new bibliographic tools or methods for negotiating specialized classification schemes. A mini-seminar series supplementing the more traditional use-of-the-library program can be developed for instructors as well as for other user groups. The series could revolve around a common theme and might stress the resolution of problems commonly encountered by documents users. Individual sessions might cover the publications of different levels of government, negotiation of separate documents collections arranged by specialized classification systems, and current developments such as those associated with microforms. It might be useful if librarians representing various libraries in the vicinity could participate in joint seminars and explain the differences in their collections. Such seminars would suggest the types of materials, print and nonprint, accessible through libraries in the immediate area.

In summary, the list of programs presented, although far from comprehensive, illustrates some of the possibilities at the disposal of librarians. Library staff members need to experiment with various options and find those most advantageous to their situation.

In cases where the number of library staff members assigned to "outreach" and reference programs is small, the demand for a service may outpace the supply. There may be a point beyond which the librarians may not be able, or motivated, to supply the service. In these cases, the librarians may discourage overall demand for a service or reduce the demand coming from certain segments of their constituency. It is necessary therefore to evaluate programs and to determine which ones can yield the maximum return with the least expenditure of time, resources, and personnel.

The utlimate test is whether users are willing to make repeated use of "outreach" services, whether librarians are reaching a large portion of the intended audience, and whether the information requirements of users are impacted. Consequently, it often takes time before the success of a program can be judged properly.

Marketing of "Outreach" Programs

Some writers have attributed limited use and non-use of government publications to a lack of public awareness of the potential value of documents. It has been assumed that "if faculty and students know about them, they will use them" (Ross, 1941, 19-21). Such an assumption, as noted in an earlier chapter, is questionable. Librarians may perceive their publicity of "outreach" programs as extensive and broadly based, but this may not be the case. Programs may be reaching only a small segment of the intended population—those who are already heavy and moderate users of government publications.

In 1950, Marquerite Murrell, a student at Western Reserve University, completed a thesis on increasing documents use. The study, which was descriptive rather than analytical, summarized pertinent writings from library literature and presented the author's impressions. A weakness of the study was that library objectives were not explored and publicity measures were not, related to them.

In her opinion, the purpose of publicity is to "create and hold attention" about the importance of the library in the educational program of the institution and to affect library use patterns. "Consulting the documents collection should become automatic to librarians and students when they seek additional information on a specific subject" (Murrell, 1950). Publicity measures, therefore, ought to emphasize sources—those of a timely, important, or unusual nature.

One problem traditionally associated with noncourse-related, "outreach" programs has been that often they have not attracted a large audience and that frequently those who attend are already heavy or moderate library users. Consequently, librarians may not be reaching the range of user groups desired; they may need to examine the literature of marketing and select target markets rather than make a quioxotic attempt to win every market and to be all things to all people. Librarians should distinguish among possible market segments, concentrate initially on those segments with the highest potential response, and design program to meet specific preferences.

Libraries wishing to develop programs and to offer more than just occasional on-demand services will have to gauge the level of interest, the needs, desires, and aversions of the people for whom programs are intended, and will have to identify problems which might arise. In the process, the following questions will have to be asked:

1. Does the clientele grasp how the program is positioned in relation to competing programs and *what its distinct benefits are?*
2. Do users show a preference for this program over competing offerings?
3. Do enough people indicate an intention to participate?
4. Do enough people say the program meets a need of theirs?
5. How do clientele feel about the form, quality, and accessibility of the intended program?

Once it has been decided to proceed with a program, librarians should inform the target audience about the program and its benefits. At the same time, librarians should create genuine interest and a desire to participate. After all, the purpose of "outreach" programs is to stimulate, create, and/or develop user dependency on government publications, in particular those held in libraries.

Program awareness can be created by such measures as personal contacts with the target audience, posters, brochures, and advertisments in campus newspapers and faculty newsletters. Since people encounter a large volume of advertising daily, no advertisement has more than a fraction of a second to attract and capture attention. The packaging of the advertisement and its message must therefore be distinctive. The words used must communicate program benefits in terms that are meaningful to the target audience. The total advertisment must convey one clear theme, because rarely will attention be held for a sufficient time to register more than one or two ideas. In effect, librarians should try to reach the target audience with a minimum of wasted coverage, deliver maximum exposure to the program, and demonstrate how the program addresses information requirements. Therefore, librarians should consider using specially prepared materials, brightly colored directional signs, and graphics.

Librarians should consider the spacing of the advertisement. They may want to concentrate all the exposure in a very short time period since presumably this attracts maximum attention and interest; if recall is good, the effect lasts for a short time. As an alternative, exposure might appear evenly throughout the period. This may be most effective when the target audience needs to be continuously reminded. Finally, intermittent small bursts of advertising may appear in succession with no advertising in between. This pattern creates more attention than does the concentrated approach and has the reminder advantages of the second pattern.

Whichever pattern is used, it is important to estimate the number of people encountering a particular advertisement and the number of times that the average person has been exposed during a given period. Such information suggests how successful library advertising has been and can be used in planning additional programs. Librarians will benefit from an examination of that portion of marketing research dealing with motivation and program effectiveness.

COLLECTION ANALYSIS

It may be that depository libraries own the majority of publications requested by their clientele, but that these items are not always on the shelves at the time of immediate need. User satisfaction, therefore, is based on more variables than just the number of titles held. Librarians should examine their documents delivery capability; their ability to answer reference queries based on the immediate collection and to retrieve sources requested. In order to study delivery capability, they can generate a pool of citations from indexes, representative of the actual needs of library documents users. The sample would reflect different publication dates and comprise both depository and nondepository items.

Next, librarians should determine the exact percentage of citations held by the library, comparing and evaluating the different options for accessing materials not held. They might also find out if those publications held by the library are kept on the immediate premises or in a storage site, microform room, or branch library, then determining how quickly the documents can be obtained and pinpointing any problems users may encounter. In other words, they would determine whether or not the publications are on the shelf or have off-shelf status. On the basis of the findings, library staff members would discover problems in accessibility for materials supposedly held (Hernon, forthcoming).

As an alternative method, documents users might record their search patterns in diaries and note sources which they could not find. They could then mark the supposed location of missing sources on the shelf. The purpose of this exercise is to monitor the documents in demand, determine how successful users are in locating desired information sources, indicate reasons for failure in finding sources, and suggest possible ways to improve document retrieval. A detailed examination could be patterned after Urquhart & Schofield (1971, 273-276; 1972, 233-241).

Additional insights might be obtained by having documents staff members record unanswered reference questions, subject areas in which the majority of reference questions fall, the specific areas of the documents department which receive the heaviest use, and even all reference questions asked during a given time period (Hernon, 1976, 255-266). The data gathered constitute a rough indicator of traffic patterns, have value for collection evaluation and the assignment of staff members to reference desks, and suggest the more heavily requested titles for which additional copies might be needed. The recording of reference questions shows which signs and audio-visual aids might reduce the number of directional questions and also indicates the level of question difficulty.

SUMMARY

Some of the major variables affecting use of documents collections identified in this study are: librarian awareness of user needs, collection development policy of the institutional library, the speed of acqustion of newly issued publications for which the demand may be heavy, the rate of processing of new acquisitions, use of collections in which the shelves are not overcrowded and in which there is weeding of unused materials, inability of some user groups to negotiate specialized classification schemes, and the amount of time spent in finding needed information in proportion to what is found. Some of the variables affecting use can be addressed by the depository libraries themselves, whereas others should be attacked by those government agencies administering depository programs. If the Government Printing Office aided depository libraries with the "outreach" objectives of increasing user awareness and orientation to the collection, documents librarians could concentrate more on the objective of instruction in the use of documents collections.

This chapter has emphasized programs which libraries can explore. The Government Printing Office could help the libraries if it were to curb numerous revisions and alterations in the Superintendent of Documents Classificiation Scheme; initiate a publicity campaign to inform the general public about the depository library system; and develop well-produced handouts, posters, and filmstrips explaining the depository program, the Superintendent of Documents Classification Scheme, and government produced indexes.

Government publications have gone through a state of transition from an archival background of public records administration to an emphasis on accessibility and information content. A problem suspected by one library educator is that:

> For many libraries the decision to follow the principle of archival arrangement has provided a practical way of identifying, shelving, and servicing large numbers of varied formats of government publications which do not conform to standard library practice and cannot be accessed according to traditional library concepts. However, the resulting failure to catalog, list, index, publicize, and distribute government publications on the same basis as conventional library materials raises a formidable barrier for both the document specialist and the potential user (Fry, 1977, 114).

Another library educator believes that "too many libraries tend to forget that the purpose of a government publication is to inform, to answer questions, and not to be an ignoble excuse for setting off hot discussion on organizational cataloging and administration" (Katz, 1978, p. 323).

Part of the problem may result from the fact that the alleged advantages of maintaining separate documents collections are based on supposition, practice, and historical tradition, rather than on scientific investigation. The provision of a better quality of reference service was, in large part, an after-the-fact rationale, justifying the trend toward separate collections. Since the nineteenth century, it has not been uncommon for libraries, deluged with an increasing volume of government publications (some of which were unwanted), to create separate collections where documents accumulated on the shelves with a minimum of evaluation and weeding. These libraries often lacked sufficient time and staff to process these publications as fully as they did other materials (Hernon, 1978, 31-50).

By the decade of the 1930s, there was "a far greater number and variety of interesting government publications than ever before, and a much greater demand for such material; hence the need for some special consideration" (Saville, 1940, 681). Separate collections isolated government publications from other library holdings and branded them with a stigma. Moreover, it was becoming more difficult for many libraries to include all of the publications in public card catalogs. Library patrons therefore had to become attuned to the possible relevance of government publishing to their needs and to plan search strategies accordingly. It could be hypothesized that as users of different libraries encountered a variety of classification schemes and arrangements for government publications, they experienced difficulty or confusion in the use of special collections.[2]

[2]Research might determine if library users encounter problems when publications for different levels of government are housed in various areas of the library and under different classification schemes. On the one hand, Federal publications might be found in both separate collections arranged by the Superintendent of Documents Classification Scheme and general collections arranged by Dewey or Library of Congress. On the other hand, publications of state and local governments as well as international organizations might be classified according to other specialized schemes. Libraries having such complex arrangements might find it advantageous to adopt computer retrieval and not make distinctions by levels of government.

Librarians need to view government publications as an information resource on an equal basis with books and serials, and to encourage their integration into library information services.[3] The relationship betwen the documents collection and other library collections should be that of a single resource in addressing user needs. Computer indexing and searching systems and better reference tools are likely to cure some of the problems for users, but inexperienced users will continue to have difficulty of direct access without aggressive and personalized reference service. The conclusion then must be that reference services should promote greater library user awareness of the documents collection and publicize the usefulness of information contained in government publications.

---

[3]One means for achieving this objective would be for more general reviewing sources to cover government publications.

Appendices

A. Explanation of Sample Selection

Once the pool of institutions had been identified from the "List of Depository Libraries" and grouped according to institutional control, it was determined which of the college and universities offered courses in the four disciplines as part of their highest degree offerings. This information was based on data found in *The College Blue Book: Degrees Offered by College and Subject* (1975). College catalogs for each institution were used to verify degree offerings for each discipline.

Not all of the depository institutions offered the four social science disciplines as part of their highest degree offerings. Therefore, the number of possible institutions was greatly reduced. Following are the criteria used for the stratified random sample of the cells (see Table 3.2 for the seventeen institutions surveyed):

1. The private baccalaureate institutions were arranged in order of enrollments, divided into three equal strata, and one institution selected from each stratum. In this way the three institutions selected were representative of enrollments, which for this cell varied from 561 to 3,253.

2. The private master's-level institutions generally had graduate programs in disciplines such as divinity or education. None of them had graduate degree programs in all four disciplines. Therefore, the institutions were selected according to whether they offered: (a) Master's degrees

in more than one of the specified departments [Butler University[1]] ; (b) a graduate degree in one of the departments [John Carroll University[2]] ; and (c) no graduate degrees in the specified departments. The third pattern was incorporated into the research design because this pattern was prevalent among the institutions in this cell.

3. Not all of the private doctorate-granting institutions offered doctorates in all four disciplines. Before sampling, those providing doctorates were arranged into "research" and "nonresearch"-oriented centers, as categorized by the Carnegie Commission on Higher Education (1973, p. v). The University of Notre Dame was selected because it was the only "nonresearch" institution which offered doctorates in all four disciplines. The other two institutions selected constituted "research" centers.

4. As only two institutions fell into the category of public baccalaureate level, both of these were represented in the study.

5. A random sample was taken of those public master's-level institutions offering master's degrees in all four disciplines. Two of the institutions, Eastern Illinois University and Central Michigan University, had specialized degrees between the master's and doctorate, but not in the disciplines under study. These two institutions were more similar to the master's than the doctorate degree programs and, therefore, have been included in the master's category.

6. Similar to the categorization for private doctoral-granting institutions, the public doctorate institutions were stratified into "research" and "nonresearch" oriented centers. Two of the research institutions were selected along with one nonresearch oriented center.

In summary, depository institutions comprise the primary sampling unit. Specific departments representing the social sciences were chosen, and all full-time faculty within these specified departments were surveyed. See Table A-1 for the depiction of the sampling frame.

[1]This institution has specialized degrees between the master's and doctorate. However, it is more similar to the master's than the doctorate degree programs and, therefore, has been included in this category. According to the Registrar, Butler University has graduate studies in economics and history.

[2]According to the Registrar, John Carroll University offers graduate studies in history.

Table A-1   Sampling Frame for the Study

Private Institutions	Name of Department	Number of Full-Time Faculty
Hanover College	Economics	3
	History	3
	Political Science	3
	Sociology	3
Ohio Wesleyan University	Economics	6
	History	6
	Government and International Studies	4
	Sociology	5
Principia College	Economics	2
	History	3
	Political Science	2
	Sociology	3
Butler University	Economics	5
	History	6
	Political Science	2
	Sociology	4
John Carroll University	Economics	10
	History	9
	Political Science	5
	Sociology	8
Valparaiso University	Economics	4
	History	6
	Political Science	5
	Sociology	6
Case Western University	Economics	8
	History	9
	Political Science	6
	Sociology	12
Northwestern University	Economics	27
	History	30
	Political Science	28
	Sociology	19
University of Notre Dame	Economics	21
	History	15
	Political Science	20
	Sociology	20

Table A-1 *Continued*

Public Institutions	Name of Department	Number of Full-Time Faculty
Indiana State University, Evansville	Economics	2
	History	4
	Political Science	3
	Sociology	4
Indiana University, Kokomo	Economics	2
	History[1]	3
	Political Science	2
	Sociology	2
Central Michigan University	Economics	15
	History	18
	Political Science	16
	Sociology	30
Eastern Illinois University	Economics	12
	History	16
	Political Science	10
	Sociology	13
Western Illinois University	Economics	15
	History	25
	Political Science	21
	Sociology	22
Indiana University, Bloomington	Economics	22
	History	50
	Political Science	38
	Sociology	37
Michigan State University	Economics	35
	History	32
	Political Science	25
	Sociology	35
Southern Illinois University	Economics	18
	History	21
	Political Science	25
	Sociology	17
Total		918

[1]There were no formal, separate social science departments at Indiana University, Kokomo. The subject disciplines were taught as part of the Division of Social and Behavioral Sciences. However, individual faculty were known as economists, historians, political scientists, and sociologists.

B. Interviewing

A mail questionnaire enabled the author to survey a large sample of social scientists in academic institutions in a four-state area. However, this method alone would not permit probing deeply into the responses given by the faculty members. Given the exploratory nature of the investigation, it was essential that certain questionnaire items be pursued further. Interviewing, therefore, was used as a supplemental technique to clarify responses of the social scientists, to obtain additional insights into the role that government information played in meeting their professional needs, to analyze why use patterns at "maverick" institutions differ from those at schools having similar control and highest degree offered, and to determine whether or not nonrespondents are indeed non-users of government publications. A secondary purpose of interviewing was to serve as a validity and reliability check on questionnaire findings.

To determine reliability over time, the author asked interview subjects how often they use the library's collection of government publications, from which levels of government they consult publications, and the age of the publications used. The responses to these questions were then compared with those of the questionnaire. Another cross-check on reliability was the fact that questionnaire responses served as a starting point for the interviews.[1] The author, for

---

[1] Given the primary objective of the interviews and the fact that they were only loosely based on questionnaire items, statistical tests for reliability were not performed. Two to six months had elapsed since the respondents had completed the questionnaires, and they rarely recalled the specific contents of the questionnaires. Comparing interview with questionnaire responses did indicate consistency in responses over time.

example, could probe the questionnaire item about whether or not the interview subject had used a computerized search system for tapping government information.

The interviewing phase of the investigation did not begin until after the responses to the questionnaire had been analyzed. On the basis of questionnaire responses, six institutions (one from each of the cells depicted in Table 3-2 were selected for interviews. Four of the institutions were selected on the basis of their proximity to Indiana University, Bloomington. The remaining two were chosen because their faculty members exhibit use patterns different from their counterparts at other institutions having similar control and degree offerings. At the first institution, only two social scientists did not return completed questionnaires, while all of the respondents make some use of government publications housed in the library. For the other institutions in the same cell, not all the respondents use the library's documents collection. Since local government sponsorship of municipal research was confined to one institution and since faculty members there make use of data bases, that school was also selected for interviewing. The purpose of interviewing at these two "maverick" institutions was to determine the reasons why these social scientists stand out from their counterparts at institutions having similar control and degree offerings.

The interview sample consisted of the six institutions and social scientists from their departments of economics, history, political science, and sociology. The initial intention was to interview three social scientists per department on the basis of their (1) heavy or moderate documents use, (2) limited use or non-use of documents, and (3) non-response to the questionnaire. However, some of the baccalaureate- and master's-granting institutions have small staffs, with only two or three faculty members assigned to a particular discipline. When this circumstance arose, the author interviewed all the social scientists in the discipline, regardless of their frequency of documents use; in some cases, they had all replied to the questionnaire.

A total of sixty-eight social scientists participated in the interviews, and they represented both public and private institutions with degree offerings ranging from the baccalaureate to the doctorate. Some seventeen (25 percent) of the interview subjects are economists; eighteen (26.5 percent), historians; sixteen (23.5 percent), political scientists; and seventeen (25 percent), sociologists. Of these sixty-eight faculty members, fifteen (22.1 percent) were nonrespondents to the questionnaire.

The fifteen interview subjects who had not responded to the questionnaire were interviewed to determine why they did not participate and if nonresponse signified non-use of government publications. The primary reasons for nonresponse are that these social scientists feel that they cannot spare the time to complete a lengthy questionnaire or that they feel the investigator is not interested in their opinions, since their use of the library's documents collection is infrequent. Only one-third of the nonrespondents do not use government publications; the others represent heavy (3), moderate (3), and limited (4) users of government publications. This finding supports that of Chapter 4—that the study was representative of the different categories for frequency of documents use.

During the latter part of March 1978, the author wrote to the social scientists reiterating the purpose of the study, indicating the dates in April when he would be visiting their institutions, and requesting alternative times for interviews. An interview schedule was devised from the requested information, and approximately one-half an hour was allotted between interviews so that the investigator could review and expand the notes generated from the sessions.

Whenever a faculty member did not respond to the request for an interview, another member of the department was selected who exhibited similar use patterns, and he was requested for an interview. In some cases, the author had to schedule interview appointments while he was visiting the institutions. Therefore, it was not uncommon for him to note office hours and to visit faculty members during one of these times. Social scientists, as a whole, were very generous with their time, even when the investigator encountered them in their offices during times unscheduled for office hours.

Library staff members were not visited during the interview phase of the study, because some limited users and non-users of the documents collection do not want the library staff members to know about their infrequent use. One social scientist appeared nervous during the first part of the interview and confessed apprehension that the author might report him to the library staff members as a non-user of government publications. He seemed reassured when it was explained to him that this would not happen and that his comments would not be identified by institution. He then proceeded to explain his reasons for non-use. On the basis of his and certain other interviews, the author has assumed that the pledge of confidentiality helped to ease apprehension about the purpose of the interviews and aided the data-collection process.[2]

---

[2] Another reason for not identifying the six interview sites by name is that at one of them, several social scientists complained about the unsatisfactory service provided by library staff members.

C. Pretest

Some of the five institutions selected for the pretest and depicted in Table C-1 did not have the four social science departments as part of their highest degree offerings. The institutions were selected, rather, on the basis of their close proximity to the Graduate Library School, Indiana University, or of the investigator knowing a librarian at that institution. None of the institutions represented in the actual survey were included; therefore, both faculty and library questionnaires were pretested. The cell "private baccalaureate" was excluded as the study sample had only two institutions for this cell; both of these were in the study itself.

Questionnaires in the form of interviews were administered personally by the author or a librarian at the institutions. Interviews were considered preferable to a mail survey as faculty members, for a variety of reasons, might have

Table C-1   Depiction of Pretest Institutions

Type of Institution	Highest Degree Offering		
	B.A.	M.A.	Ph.D.
Private	Anderson College	DePauw University	University of Dayton
Public	—	Governors State University	Purdue University

been unwilling to critique a mail questionnaire. A mail pretest might have provided insights into return rates but not have questioned phraseology and content. In interviews faculty members were encouraged to be critical and to verbalize their opinions.

In order to gain a broad range of answers, the author administered interviews individually to faculty members at two of the institutions. At the remaining three institutions, librarians who were personally known to the author gathered faculty members and administered the questionnaires in groups.

Fifty faculty members and five librarians comprised the pretest sample. Ten faculty members were selected from among the specified social science departments at each institution. The exact proportion of faculty from each department was left to the cooperating librarian to determine; however, each department was represented by two or more faculty members. As it was difficult to arrange a satisfactory time for ten faculty members to meet, interviews had to be scheduled at several different times. Librarians were cautioned that they should schedule a minimum of two faculty members per session, as one purpose of these encounters was to provoke verbal interaction.

All faculty participants were asked to complete questionnaires. Afterwards, the investigator or librarian went over each question with faculty members and encouraged them to point out unclear items and pertinent categories, if need be. Faculty members were encouraged to raise questions so that as many unclarities as possible could be eliminated.

Previous to the session, the author discussed the faculty questionnaire with the librarian so that this person understood the intent of each question. Whenever faculty members raised alternative interpretations, it was noted.

In summary, the pretest procedure enabled the author to participate in some of the interviews and allowed a person without previous knowledge of the study to administer questionnaires. The results indicated the strengths and weaknesses of the survey instruments; at the same time, the pretest had safeguards against any bias possibly caused by the presence of the author during interviews.

On the basis of the comments made by faculty members and librarians, both the faculty and librarian questionnaires were revised and shortened. After it was determined that the survey instruments were of acceptable quality, questionnaires were mailed to the entire sample.

D. Faculty Questionnaire

SURVEY OF FACULTY USE AND NON-USE OF
GOVERNMENT PUBLICATIONS

Background Information

1. Estimate the percentage of your working time involved with:

    a. teaching _____   d. other (please specify)
    b. research or scholarly   _____
        writing _____
    c. administrative duties _____

2. Are the courses that you teach primarily at the (check as many as apply)

    a. freshman and sophomore   e. other (if so, specify)?
        level _____?   _____
    b. junior and senior   f. I do not teach regularly
        level _____?   _____
    c. graduate (doctorate)
        level _____?

3. In the space provided below, select, from among the categories in the accompanying sheet (see p. 149), the area of specialty reflected in your teaching.

4. Are the currently engaged in, or have you recently completed (within the past three years), a research project?

   a. sponsored:[1]   yes _____ no _____
   b. nonsponsored: yes _____ no _____

5. If you research is or was sponsored, would you please identify the funding source as to:

   a. federal government _____   d. private foundation _____
   b. state government _____   e. industry or business _____
   c. local government _____   f. your own institution _____

Library Use

6. Estimate how many times you used the resources of the college or university library last year.

   a. more than 20 _____   d. 6-10 _____
   b. 16-20 _____   e. 1-5 _____
   c. 11-15 _____   f. 0 _____

7. Estimate how many times last year you used government publications[2] (those of Federal, state, and/or municipal government) located in the college or university library.

   a. more than 20 _____   d. 6-10 _____
   b. 16-20 _____   e. 1-5 _____
   c. 11-15 _____   f. 0 _____

8. If you answered "e" or "f" to question 7, please indicate why your use is infrequent. Check as many as apply. (If you responded to items "a," "b," "c," or "d," move to the next question.)

   a. government publishes little or nothing of value in my field _____
   b. unaware of the existence of such materials at the library _____
   c. unfamiliar with arrangement of the government publications collection _____
   d. rely on government publications located in a library other than on this campus _____

[1] A sponsored project has direct financial support from either the institution itself or an external source, a government agency or private foundation.

[2] A government publication means information matter which has been published as an individual document at government expense, or as required by law.

e. obtain personal copies of government publications _____
f. the amount of time expended in trying to find relevant information in government publications is out of proportion to what I find _____
g. the library staff members provide minimal assistance in use of government publications _____
h. rely on secretary, student, or research assistants to gather any needed government publications _____
i. the desired government publication is available in the library only on microform _____
j. microformed government publications are separated from the rest of the government publications collection _____
k. was not a member of this faculty last year _____
l. other (please specify) _____

If you responded only to "f" in question 7, skip to number 24 (if you responded to "a," "b," "c," "d," or "e" in question 7, move to question 9)

9. Do you consult government publications in your field to obtain any of the following? (Check as many options as apply.)

a. current events and issues of interest _____
b. census or normative data _____
c. information of historical value _____
d. research and technical reports _____
e. resources that may be of value to students _____
f. grant information _____
g. recreational reading material _____
h. other (please specify) _____

10. In using government publications, how often do you ask library staff members for assistance?

a. never _____   c. frequently _____
b. sometimes _____   d. always _____

11. Are you reluctant to ask library staff for assistance in using the government publications collection?

a. yes _____   (if yes, move to question 12)
b. no _____   (if no, respond to 13)

12. If you answered "yes" to question 11, check those options which contribute to the reluctance:

    a. the staff is discourteous _____
    b. the staff provides unsatisfactory service _____
    c. the staff appears not well informed _____
    d. the staff appears too busy to have time to deal with your question _____
    e. consultation with staff does not lead to the desired government publication _____
    f. your question may seem too elementary and you ought to know the answer _____
    g. other (please specify) _____

13. For what kinds of assistance do you ask the library staff? (Check as many as apply.)

    a. help in locating a specific government publication _____
    b. reference assistance, i.e., aid in finding materials or information to answer a specific question or solve some problem on which you are working _____
    c. assistance in finding government publications not located on the shelf _____
    d. assistance in locating government publications not held by the library
       _____
    e. help in ordering for the library a government publication not contained in the collection _____
    f. other (please specify) _____

14. If you do not generally require assistance, how do you locate the government publications you need? (Check as many as apply.)

    a. by consulting the public card catalog _____
    b. by consulting indexes of government publications _____
    c. by finding citations to government publications in the general literature or special bibliographies in your subject field _____
    d. by finding references in newspapers _____
    e. by browsing in areas of the collection relevant to your interests
       _____
    f. by receiving citations to government publications from the library staff _____
    g. by relying on sources already familiar to you _____
    h. other (please specify) _____

15. If you are able to find materials in the government publications collection on your own, how did you learn to do so?

    a. through a trial-and-error process in actually using the collection _____

    b. self-instruction, by reading manuals or guides to the use of government publications _____

    c. informal instruction from the library staff _____

    d. formal course work _____

    e. other (please specify) _____

16. Do you use publications of any of the following? (Check as many options as apply and order them in terms of frequency of use with 1 for the greatest use, 2 for the next greatest, etc.)

    a. federal government _____   d. foreign governments _____

    b. state government _____   e. United Nations and other inter-

    c. municipal government _____   national agencies _____

17. Do you use a search system (computerized or manual) that accesses government information contained in bibliographic or numeric data bases? (If no, proceed to 19.)

    a. yes _____

    b. no _____

18. If you answered "yes" to question 17, specify the computerized search system used. (Mark as many as apply by placing an "x" by those involving a fee-for-service and a "√" by those not involving a charge.)

    a. AcCIS (on line information retrieval to Congressional Information Service publications) _____

    b. CAIN/AGRICOLA (Agricultural On Line Access) _____

    c. ERIC Search *(Resources in Education, Current Index to Journals in Education)* _____

    d. MEDLINE _____

    e. NTISearch (National Technical Information Service) _____

    f. SSIE (Smithsonian Science Information Exchange) _____

    g. census tapes (U.S. Bureau of the Census) _____

    h. other (please specify) _____

_____

19. If you use federal publications, please check the following guides and indexes, if any, which you consult:

    a. *Air Pollution Abstracts* _____

    b. *American Statistics Index* _____

    c. *CIS* (Congressional Information Service) *Index* _____

    d. *CIS US Serial Set Index* _____

    e. *Declassified Documents Catalog* _____

    f. *ERIC Resources in Education* _____

    g. *Government Reports Announcement & Index* _____

    h. historical indexes which include "Documents Catalog" *(Catalog of the Public Documents of the 53rd to 76th Congress and All Departments of the Government . . .),* "Tables and Index" *(Tables of, and Annotated Index to the Congressional Series of U.S. Public Documents, 15th to 52nd Congress),* Ames' *Comprehensive Index to the Publications of the U.S. Government, 1881-1893,* Poore's *Descriptive Catalog of the Government Publications of the U.S., Sept. 5, 1774-March 4, 1881,* and *Checklist of U.S. Public Documents* _____

    i. *Index Medicus* _____

    j. *Index to U.S. Government Periodicals* _____

    k. *Monthly Catalog of U.S. Government Publications* _____

    l. *Nuclear Science Abstracts/Atomindex* _____

    m. *PAIS* (Public Affairs Information Service) *Bulletin* _____

    n. *Scientific Technical Aerospace Reports* _____

    o. *Selected U.S. Government Publications* _____

    p. *Selected Water Resources Abstracts* _____

    q. *Technical Abstracts Bulletin* _____

    r. *Transdex* (index to JPRS publications) _____

    s. U.S. Geological Survey Publications indexes _____

    t. other (please specify)_____

        _____

20. In addition to the guides and indexes noted in question 19, do you locate federal publications by any of the following? (Check as many as apply.)

    a. checking newspapers _____

    b. contacting federal agencies _____

    c. being on mailing lists of federal agencies _____

    d. drawing on resources of associations _____

    e. drawing on resources of professional societies _____

    f. finding citations in the general literature or special bibliographies in your subject field _____

    g. receiving citations from colleagues _____
    h. receiving assistance from librarians _____
    i. browsing selection aids such as *Selected U.S. Government Publications* _____

    j. other (please specify) _____

21. If you use state publications, please check the method(s) that you use to locate materials:

    a. consulting *Monthly Checklist of State Publications* _____
    b. consulting *Legislative Research Checklist* _____
    c. consulting individual state checklists _____
    d. checking newspapers _____
    e. contacting state agencies _____
    f. drawing on resources of associations _____
    g. drawing on resources of professional societies _____
    h. finding citations in the general literature or special bibliographies in your subject field _____
    i. being on mailing lists of state agencies _____
    j. receiving citations from colleagues _____
    k. receiving assistance from librarians _____
    l. other (please specify) _____

22. If you use municipal publications, please check the method(s) that you use to locate materials:

    a. using *Index to Current Urban Documents* _____
    b. consulting individual city checklists _____
    c. checking newspapers _____
    d. contacting municipal agencies _____
    e. being on the mailing lists of municipal agencies _____
    f. drawing on resources of associations _____
    g. drawing on resources of professional societies _____
    h. finding citations in the general literature or special bibliographies in your subject field _____
    i. receiving citations from colleagues _____
    j. receiving assistance from librarians _____
    k. other (please specify) _____

23. Generally how old are the government publications you most frequently consult? (Mark only *one* response.)

    a. less than a year old _____   d. 6-10 years old _____
    b. 1-3 years old _____   e. over 10 years old _____
    c. 4-5 years old _____   f. no set pattern; age varies _____

Questions 24 and 25 are to be completed only by those faculty not using government publications.

24. Are there any particular aspects of the library goverment publications collection and its organization which you feel are a cause of frustration or confusion?

    a. yes _____   b. no _____

25. If you answered "yes" to question 24 check those following options which contribute to the frustration or confusion. (If you answered "no," skip to question 26.)

    a. government publications are not housed together in one part of the library _____
    b. government publications are not housed together near the main reference collection _____
    c. the public card catalog does not list all the government publications _____
    d. the classification scheme(s) is confusing _____
    e. government publications are too crowded on the shelves _____
    f. needed government publications are not on the shelves _____
    g. it is difficult to determine which government publications the library does and does not have _____
    h. the library does not publish guides explaining the government publications collection _____
    i. the library staff is discourteous _____
    j. the library staff provides unsatisfactory service _____
    k. the library staff appears not well informed _____
    l. the staff appears too busy to have time to deal with your question _____
    m. consultation with library staff does not lead to the desired government publication _____
    n. the library has few of the government publications needed _____
    o. other (please specify) _____

_____

Questions 26 through 29 are to be completed by all survey respondents.

26. Are you currently engaged in, or have you recently completed within the past year, a scholarly activity intended for publication, which cites a government publication(s) in the bibliography or footnotes?

    a. yes _____   b. _____

27. What method(s) does your library employ to enhance faculty and student awareness of important government publications? (Check as many options as apply.)

  a. library lectures conducted through the classroom _____
  b. tours _____
  c. cassette tapes _____
  d. brochures _____
  e. special seminars _____
  f. term paper clinic _____
  g. credit course on library usage _____
  h. noncredit course on library usage _____
  i. workshops _____
  j. preparation of bibliographic guides to specific disciplines _____
  k. preparation of manuals and handouts _____
  l. address departmental meetings _____
  m. visit faculty members individually _____
  n. set up displays _____
  o. maintain browsing areas _____
  p. enter them in public card catalog _____
  q. maintain documents bulletin board _____
  r. employ signs _____
  s. offer current awareness services (establishment of a system for reviewing new publications and information relating to the needs of specific faculty and the dissemination of this data through newsletters, etc.) _____
  t. other (please specify) _____
  u. no regular program employed _____

28. How have you made your students aware of the government publications collection at the university or college library?

  a. formally, through specific class assignments _____
  b. by having government publications on required or suggested reading lists _____
  c. informally, by suggesting the collection as a valuable source of information _____
  d. by having a librarian provide specialized instruction in the use of the library _____
  e. by referring students to a library _____
  f. have never had occasion to mention the collection to students _____

29. Specify the method of instruction you prefer the library to undertake for assisting students in using government publications. (Mark *only one* response.)

    a. formal, credit course _____
    b. formal, non-credit course _____
    c. incorporation of instruction into existing subject bibliographic courses _____
    d. instruction through library class lectures, tours, term paper clinics, or reference rap sessions _____
    e. no instruction required _____
    f. other (please specify) _____

Please return completed questionnaire to: Peter Hernon
                                             Research Center for Library
                                                and Information Science
                                             Graduate Library School
                                             Indiana University
                                             Bloomington, Indiana 47401

Categories for Questions 3 (p. 140)

ECONOMICS:

    Comparative economic systems
    Econometrics and statistics
    Economic theory
    History
    Industrial organization
    International economics
    Labor and human resources development
    Planning
    Public finance
    Urban economics
    Other (please specify)

HISTORY:

    African
    American
    Ancient
    Asian

English
Latin American
Medieval
Modern
Russian, Soviet, and Eastern European
Other (please specify)

POLITICAL SCIENCE:

American politics
Comparative politics
International relations
Law
Public administration
Public policy
Political theory
Other (please specify)

SOCIOLOGY:

Criminology
Deviance
Social organization
Social psychology
Theory
Urban sociology
Sociology of an area
  (i.e., family, religion,
  medicine, science, etc.)
Other (please specify)

SOCIAL WORK:

Please specify
the area

ANTHROPOLOGY:

Please specify the
area

E. Analysis of Faculty Respondents

The distribution of respondents by department is depicted in Table E-1. A comparison of returns per institution to the number of full-time faculty members at their respective institutions indicates that all of the institutions except three had return rates of at least 72 percent. The exceptions, all private institutions, had return rates of 61.9 percent (Ohio Wesleyan University), 68.7 percent (John Carroll University), and 61.5 percent (Northwestern University). Further examination of the responses at these three institutions reveals that the return rates for three specific departments (sociology at Ohio Wesleyan University, history at John Carroll University, and sociology at Northwestern University) were less than fifty percent.

As Table 4-1 suggests, any impact caused by the low response rate from these three departments has been lessened by the extensive participation of faculty members at other institutions having similar highest degree offerings and institutional control. There was a response of 54.5 percent from sociologists at private baccalaureate granting institutions, of 76.2 percent from historians at private master's-level institutions, and of 70.6 percent from sociologists at private doctorate-granting institutions.

When the responses for each department were collapsed to reflect faculty participation according to highest degree offered and institutional control (i.e., private baccalaureate, private master's, and private doctoral), as represented in Table 4-1 only the category of private doctoral institutions had less than a 72 percent return; the response for this category was 69 percent.

151

Table E-1   Faculty Respondents by Institution and Department

Institutions (Public)	Department	Number of Full-Time Faculty	
		Total	Respondents
Indiana State University	Economics	2	2
	History	4	3
	Political Science	3	3
	Sociology	4	4
Indiana University, Kokomo	Economics	2	2
	History	3	2
	Political Science	2	2
	Sociology	2	2
Central Michigan University	Economics	15	12
	History	18	16
	Political Science	16	9
	Sociology	30	22
Eastern Illinois University	Economics	12	11
	History	16	11
	Political Science	10	8
	Sociology	13	7
Western Illinois University	Economics	15	9
	History	25	20
	Political Science	21	14
	Sociology	22	17
Indiana University, Bloomington	Economics	22	15
	History	50	36
	Political Science	38	28
	Sociology	37	29
Michigan State University	Economics	35	30
	History	32	25
	Political Science	25	17
	Sociology	35	30
Southern Illinois University	Economics	18	12
	History	21	16
	Political Science	25	18
	Sociology	17	14
Total		590	446

Institutions (Private)	Department	Number of Full-Time Faculty	
		Total	Respondents
Hanover College	Economics	3	3
	History	3	2
	Political Science	3	3
	Sociology	3	2
Ohio Wesleyan University	Economics	6	3
	History	6	5
	Government and International Studies	4	3
	Sociology	5	2
Principia College	Economics	2	1
	History	3	3
	Political Science	2	2
	Sociology	3	2
Butler University	Economics	5	4
	History	6	6
	Political Science	2	2
	Sociology	4	4
John Carroll University	Economics	10	6
	History	9	4
	Political Science	5	4
	Sociology	8	8
Valparaiso University	Economics	4	3
	History	6	6
	Political Science	5	4
	Sociology	6	5
Case University University	Economics	8	7
	History	9	5
	Political Science	6	4
	Sociology	12	10
Northwestern University	Economics	27	15
	History	30	23
	Political Science	28	18
	Sociology	19	8

Table E-1 *Continued*

Institutions (Private)	Department	Number of Full-Time Faculty	
		Total	Respondents
University of Notre Dame	Economics	21	16
	History	15	12
	Government and International Studies	20	14
	Sociology	20	18
Total		328	237
Total for both private and public institutions		918	683

F. Library Questionnaire

1. Has your library staff undertaken a study of faculty use of the government documents collection?

    a. yes _____   b. no _____

    If yes, a copy of it would be greatly appreciated.

2. In addition to the Federal documents collection, check if your library systematically collects publications of:

    a. state government _____
    b. municipal government

        _____
    c. governments of foreign countries _____

    d. United National and other international agencies _____
    e. none of the above _____

    If "e" is marked, move to question 6.

3. If you indicated in question 2 that your library systematically gathers state publications, check those which you collect. Mark as many options as apply.

    a. your own state _____
    b. your region _____
    c. selected states from
        different regions _____

    d. every state _____
    e. other (please specify)
        _____

4. If you indicated in question 2 that your library systematically gathered municipal publications, check the publications which you collect. Mark as many options as apply.

    a. your own city _____
    b. other cities in the
        state _____
    c. selected other cities
        in the region _____

    d. selected cities throughout the
        nation_____
    e. other (please specify)
        _____

5. Has your library been designated as a depostiory for the publications of any of the governments listed in question 2?

		Yes	No
a.	state		
b.	municipal		
c.	United Nations and other international agencies		

6. Does your library supplement its holdings of government publications by participation in a cooperative depository or consortium such as Center for Research Libraries?

    a. yes _____

    b. no _____

7. In addition to the depository items received through the Superintendent of Documents, has your library been designated as a depository for the publications of any of the following?

    a. Bureau of the Census _____
    b. Department of Housing and
        Urban Development _____
    c. U.S. Geological Survey _____

    d. Other (please specify)
        _____

8. Are the documents kept in any of the following areas? (Check appropriate categories and elaborate if necessary on a separate sheet.)

	Federal	State	Municipal
a. in a separate collection			
b. incorporated into the general collection			
c. in a pamphlet file			
d. a combination of the above (please specify by letter)			

9. Specify the number of FTE personnel servicing (processing and providing reference service) documents:

Total _____: Professional _____; Clerical _____; Paraprofessional _____.

10. Do reference librarians also service the collection?

a. yes _____   b. no _____

11. How does the library classify documents? (If necessary, elaborate on a separate sheet.)

	SUDOC	DEWEY	LC	Other (please specify)
a. Federal				
b. state				
c. municipal				

12. Estimate the percentage of the Federal documents categories your library selectes.

a. designation as regional depository _____
b. over 90% _____
c. 70-89% _____
d. 50-69% _____
e. 30-49% _____
f. 10-29% _____
g. under 10% _____

13. Are any catalog cards for government publications placed in the library's public catalog? (If no, proceed to 15.)

    a. yes _____   b. no _____

14. If you answered "yes" to question 13, estimate what percentage of documents received are cataloged?

	Federal	State	Municipal
a. over 90%			
b. 70-89%			
c. 50-69%			
d. 30-49%			
e. 10-29%			
f. under 10%			

15. In using government publications, how often do these faculty ask library staff members for assistance?

	DEPARTMENT			
	Economics	History	Political Science	Sociology
a. never				
b. sometimes				
c. frequently				
d. always				
e. no opinion				

16. Does your library have a regular program for informing faculty of new publications and services available for government publications? (If no, proceed to 18.)

    a. yes _____   b. no _____

17. What method(s) does your library employ to enhance faculty and student awareness of important government publications? (Check as many options as apply.)

    a. library lectures conducted through the classroom _____

    b. tours _____

    c. cassette tapes _____

    d. brochures _____

    e. special seminars _____

    f. term paper clinic _____

    g. credit course on library usage _____

    h. noncredit course on library usage _____

    i. workshops _____

    j. preparation of bibliographic guides to specific disciplines _____

    k. preparation of manuals and handouts _____

    l. address departmental meetings _____

    m. visit faculty members individually _____

    n. set up displays _____

    o. maintain browsing areas _____

    p. enter them in public card catalog _____

    q. maintain documents bulletin board _____

    r. employ signs _____

    s. offer current awareness services (establishment of a system for reviewing new publications and information relating to the needs of specific faculty and the dissemination of this data through newsletters, etc.) _____

    t. other (please specify) _____

18. If the government publications are kept in a separate collection, where is the collection located in relation to the reference collection?

    a. on the same floor _____   d. other (please specify)

    b. on another floor _____   _____

    c. in another building _____

19. Do you circulate documents to faculty?

    a. yes _____   b. no _____

20. If you issue a copy of the departmental annual report, have a copy of the latest *Biennial Report of Depository Libraries* to the Government Printing

Office, or have available statistics on documents circulation, it would be appreciated if you would make them available.

Please return completed questionnaire to: Peter Hernon
Graduate Library School
Indiana University
Bloomington, Indiana 47401

Bibliography

ARTICLES IN JOURNALS

Boast, C., and Nyberg, C. "The Monthly Catalog, July 1976-August 1977: Observations, Evaluation, Congratulations." *Government Publications Review,* 5 (1978): 167-176.

Danielson, D. "United Nations Documents at Northwestern University." *Illinois Libraries,* 55 (March 1973): 142-146.

Fry, B. M. "Government Publications and the Library: Implications for Change." *Government Publications Review,* 4 (1977): 111-117.

Harrison, J. J. "United States Congressional Publication Indexing: Statistical Comparisons between the CIS/Index and the Monthly Catalog." *Government Publications Review,* 5 (1978): 273-283.

Haynes, F. and Coykendall, F. "Documents Can Be News." *Wilson Library Bulletin,* 17 (March 1943): 544.

Hernon, P. "Academic Library Reference Service for the Publications of Municipal, State, and Federal Government: An Historical Perspective Spanning the Years up to 1962." *Government Publications Review,* 5 (1978): 31-50.

Hernon, P. "An Approach to Teaching Documents," *Government Publications Review,* forthcoming.

Hernon, P. "State 'Documents to the People,'" *Government Publications Review,* 3 (1976): 255-266.

Hernon, P., and Williams, Sara Lou. "University Faculty and Federal Documents." *Government Publications Review,* 3 (1976): 93-108.

McCaghy, D., and Purcell, G. R. "Faculty Use of Government Publications." *College and Research Libraries,* 33 (January 1972): 7-12.

McClure, R. "Indexing U.S. Government Periodicals: Analysis and Comments." *Government Publications Review,* 5 (1978), 409-421.

McIlvaine, B. "University of Connecticut Faculty Use of Government Documents." *Connecticut Libraries,* 17 (1975): 49-51.

"PAIS Selection Policy," *PAIS Bulletin,* 63 (1977), vii-ix.

Reynolds, C. J. "Discovering the Government Documents Collection in Libraries." *RQ,* 14 (Spring 1975): 228-231.

Ross, E. "Documents Publicity in Colleges." *Illinois Libraries,* 23 (June 1941): 19-21.

Saville, M. "Government Publications—What Shall We Do with Them? *The Library Journal,* 65 (September 1, 1940): 681.

Schwartzkopf, L. C. "The Depository Library Program and Access by the Public to Official Publications of the United States Government." *Government Publications Review,* 5 (1978): 147-156.

Stein, J. W. "Introducing Public Administration." *Teaching Political Science,* 3 (October 1975): 98-105.

Tobin, J. "A Study of Library 'Use Studies.'" *Information Storage and Retrieval,* 10 (March-April 1974): 101-113.

Urquhart, J. A., and Schofield, J. L. "Measuring Readers' Failure at the Shelf." *Journal of Documentation,* 27 (1971): 273-276.

Urquhart, J. A., "Measuring Readers' Failure at the Shelf in Three University Libraries." *Journal of Documentation,* 28 (1972): 233-241.

Waldo, M. "An Historical Look at the Debate over How to Organize Federal Government Documents in Depository Libraries." *Government Publications Review,* 4 (1977): 319-329.

Weech, T. L. "The Use of Government Publications: A Selected Review of the Literature." *Government Publications Review,* 5 (1978): 177-184.

Whitbeck, G. W., Hernon, P., and Richardson, J. V. "The Federal Depository Library System: A Descriptive Analysis." *Government Publications Review,* 5 (1978), 253-267.

White, M. "The Communications Behavior of Academic Economists in Research Phases." *Library Quarterly,* 45 (October 1975): 337-354.

Wilson, M. H. "Faculty Use of Government Publications at Trinity University." *Texas Library Journal,* 49 (May 1973): 76-80.

BOOKS

Boyd, A. M., and Rips, R. *United States Government Publications.* New York: H.W. Wilson Co., 1949.

Buckland, M. K. *Book Availability and the Library User.* New York: Pergamon Press, 1975.

Carnegie Commission on Higher Education. *A Classification of Institutions of Higher Education.* Berkeley, CA: Carnegie Commission on Higher Education, 1973.

The College Blue Book: Degrees Offered by College and Subject. 15th ed. New York: Macmillan Info., 1975.

Glass, G. V., and Stanley, J. C. *Statistical Methods in Education and Psychology.* Englewood Cliffs, NJ: Prentice-Hall, Inc., 1970.

Information Please Almanac, 1975. New York: Simon and Schuster, 1974.

Investigation into Information Requirements of the Social Sciences. Research Report No. 1. Vol. 1. Text by Maurice B. Line, Project Head. Bath, England: Bath University of Technology, University Library, May 1971.

Jarvi, E. *Access to Canadian Government Publications in Canadian Academic and Public Libraries,* Ottawa, Ontario: Canadian Library Association, 1976.

Katz, W. A. *Introduction to Reference Work: Basic Information Sources.* Vol. 1. 3rd ed. New York: McGraw-Hill Book Co., 1978.

Lancaster, F.W. *The Measurement and Evaluation of Library Services.* Washington, DC: Information Resources Press, 1977.

Selltiz, C., Jahoda, M., Deutsch, M., and Cook, S. *Research Methods in Social Relations.* 2nd ed. New York: Holt, Rinehart and Winston, 1959.

Siegel, S. *Nonparametric Statistics for the Behavioral Sciences.* New York: McGraw-Hill Book Co., 1956.

Voigt, M. J. *Scientists' Approaches to Information.* ACRL Monograph 24. Chicago: American Library Association, 1961.

GOVERNMENT DOCUMENTS

Annual Report of The Public Printer. Fiscal Year 1973. Washington, DC: Government Printing Office, n.d.

"List of Depository Libraries as of September 1, 1975." In *Monthly Catalog of United States Government Publications,* pp. 167-193. Washington, DC: Government Printing Office, 1976.

Statistical Abstracts of the United States 1975. Washington, DC: Government Printing Office, 1975.

Statistical Abstracts of the United States 1973. Washington, DC: Government Printing Office, 1973.

U.S. Department of Health, Education and Welfare. Office of Education. *Education Directory, 1974-75: Higher Education.* Washington, DC: Government Printing Office, 1975.

U.S. Government Printing Office. *Guidelines for the Depository Library System, as Adopted by the Depository Library Council to the Public Printer,* October 18, 1977.

THESES

DeVelbiss, E. M. "A Study of the Use of the Subject Card Catalog in Locating Government Documents in the University of California." M.A. thesis, University of California, 1956.

Murrell, M. "Increasing the Use of Government Publications in College Libraries." M.S. thesis, Western Reserve University, 1950.

Indexes

Author Index

167

Subject Index

Title Index

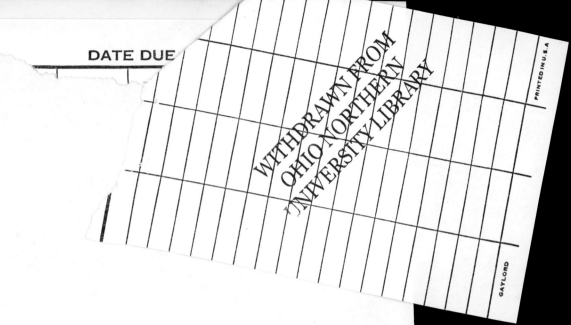